The Family That Plays Together
Fun Traditions to Strengthen Your Family

Sabrina Huyett

Ideas for your Passover or Easter tradition:

_____

_____

_____

_____

_____

Ideas for your Fourth of July tradition:

_____

_____

_____

_____

_____

Ideas for your Halloween tradition:

_____

_____

_____

_____

_____

Ideas for your Thanksgiving tradition:

_____

_____

_____

_____

_____

Ideas for your Hanukkah or Christmas tradition:

_____

_____

_____

_____

_____

Ideas for your _____ tradition:

_____

_____

_____

_____

_____

Ideas for your _____ tradition:

_____

_____

_____

_____

_____

Ideas for your _____ tradition:

_____

_____

_____

_____

_____

Ideas for your _____ tradition:

_____

_____

_____

_____

_____

Did you like what you saw?

Tell us your experiences while trying out these traditions!

Want to see more?

Send us your own original traditions to help expand the next edition of the book!

Contact us at:

funfamilytraditions.blogspot.com

funfamilytraditions@gmail.com

Table of Contents

Author's Note

In our modern society, the need for family traditions is stronger than ever. Busy schedules keep family members physically apart from each other. Technology may isolate families even while they are at home. If we're not careful, our family ties become weaker over time. Hence the need for family traditions! Family traditions range from simple to complex, from daily to once-a-year. They are rituals that bind our families together. Family traditions give a sense of identity, that "in our family, we do _____." They tie children to parents and create fond memories. When children grow up, they often lament that their parents do not keep up the traditions from their childhood. Family traditions are exciting things to children. Things they expect. Things they look forward to. A constant in a changing world. It is an opportunity for parents to pass on values. Even the simplest of family traditions sends an unspoken message to children that "_____ is important to my parents, and also to me." That blank can be "having fun," "being together," "serving others," or any number of things. Research proves that family traditions matter. The tradition of eating dinner together as a family has been shown to have positive effects in a child's life, including on academic achievement. In fact, I would say that any tradition is beneficial to the family. So if your goal is to create a strong, united family, please read on and start your own family traditions!

This book is intended to be a resource of traditions that you can incorporate in your own family. Even choosing one family tradition can have a positive effect on your family. Do not feel the need to introduce every tradition that you like at the same time. Over the course of a year, you can successfully introduce several new family traditions. Some may be keepers. Others you may decide you can do without. Just the act of trying out a tradition can be beneficial.

The idea for this book grew out of my love for my own family's traditions. We do many fun things throughout the year, and it made holidays more special and exciting. I loved talking with people about their family traditions, and when people replied that they didn't have any, I thought it was sad. I thought about how my mother copied a tradition from her childhood friend and started it in our family. I realized that although many traditions are passed down, they can also be consciously added. Thus, I decided to make this book as a resource for families.

So I talked to my friends and family. I wrote an e-mail and asked people to forward it on to as many friends as they could. I made a mass call for traditions on social networking sites. And the e-mails flooded my inbox. I have preserved the original writing of the contributors as much as possible. I like hearing their voices come through. Some changes have been made for editing and clarity. I hope you also enjoy reading these traditions in the voices of their authors. As I became acquainted with the traditions in this book, I have grown to love many of them. I hope to use some of these new traditions in my future family. I expect you will have the same experience. I love family traditions, and I hope to share some of this joy with you and your family!

How to Use This Book

You may want to read this book straight through, or you may choose to flip to a specific section. Either way will work. When you come across a tradition you like, think about how you might put it in practice. What things will you have to change in order to adapt it to your family? What else can you add to the tradition? It is important to remember that these traditions are springboards for your own ideas. You do not have to do exactly what the original family did—adapt it to *your* family.

I suggest you talk with your children before you start the new traditions. Involve them in the decision-making process! Decide as a family what you think would be fun to do. I always liked being a part of making decisions in my family. I helped influence new traditions, and made sure we kept on doing them. I would recommend choosing one or two traditions to start with. After deciding which traditions to implement, write them down so that you do not forget.

Try the traditions out once or twice, and see how they feel. If you do not like them, throw them out. You may discover that you need to make adjustments to the traditions. Add fun tweaks! After adding a few traditions, find some more. Continue until you feel that you have the right balance for your family.

Also, every tradition needs a "keeper." The keeper is the person in your family who makes sure that the tradition continues. When children are young, the parents will often be the keepers of the tradition. You'll know it's a good tradition when your children assume this role. You'll know it's a great tradition if they pass it on to your grandchildren.

You will notice that at the end of each chapter there are a few lines to write down the tradition ideas you liked. At the end of the book there is space to write out your traditions for the whole year. Please take advantage of this space to record the traditions you liked, with modifications to fit your family. It is my hope that writing them down will help you to remember them and carry them out.

I would like to thank the many people who shared their family traditions with me. Without them, this book would not have been possible. I would also like to thank Mom, Dad, Charla, Ryan, and Lisa for helping me edit. Many thanks to Spencer Greenhalgh, who spent hours upon hours doing all the formatting, and to Anneke Majors, who designed the cover. Thank you to the Stand for the Family Symposium—had my project not been accepted, I may have never completed this dream.

Birthday Traditions

...they come but once a year!

BIRTHDAY

We always go out to dinner as a family, and the birthday kid picks the place.

Lisa Nielson

My family all lives close together, so everyone comes to birthdays. Grandma makes her famous chocolate chip cookies that only she can make, and she also brings her special pudding. It is a white tapioca pudding, and it has a single nut in it. If your dish has the nut then you get a prize.

Claire

The birthday person gets to pick out their favorite sugar cereal, and chooses all of the food to be eaten that day. We switch each year between having a family birthday party and a friend birthday party.

Sabrina Huyett

Early in the morning on birthdays, my father would play "Las Mañanitas," a traditional Spanish birthday song that we sing in El Salvador, and everybody from the family would get up to sing to the birthday person. The telephone would ring like crazy while family members who lived far away called and wished the birthday person a very happy birthday. Now my children are continuing this tradition in their families.

Ana Cristina Rubio

We don't only celebrate birthdays for one day, we have birthday week! One night we go out to dinner, and a different night we make the person's favorite food for dinner, and a bunch of other special things.

Gina Woolf

On birthdays, we have the "Birthday Brigade." This is to celebrate the birthdays of people who aren't family members. Our family goes to the dollar store, picks something out, and delivers it to that person on their birthday.

Gina Woolf

For birthdays we always wake up way early and decorate the birthday persons room and make them breakfast in bed.

Jessica Scott

My family likes to give coupons as presents— homemade coupons. A popular example was the "do your chores for the week coupon."

Benjamin Jensen

For your birthday you get whatever cake you want and a giant cookie cake! We also sing a "sad birthday hymn" to the birthday person.

Linze Struiksma

Birthday

My mom takes us each on a birthday trip around the time of our birthday. We stay overnight in a motel, and then do something special together the next day. The birthday kid gets to pick out what we do. My brothers usually pick to go to the science museum, I usually choose to see a play, and my sisters usually choose shopping trips.

Sabrina Huyett

My mom and me during a birthday trip

BIRTHDAY

On birthdays, my parents give the birthday child
dollar bills. They give the same amount of dollars as
the child's age. So, on the child's tenth birthday they
receive ten dollars. Everyone else receives a single
dollar. This money is hidden under our birthday
breakfast dishes.

Ariel Bean

On our birthdays when we were little, my dad used to
go in the garage before our family parties, blow up a
bunch of balloons and put them in a big giant trash
bag. Then when everyone was singing Happy Birthday
he would sneak in and dump the bag of balloons on the
birthday girl. I always thought it was the coolest thing
ever when I was a kid.

Amanda Kidder

At birthdays, after singing and blowing the candles
out, everyone waits while the birthday person pulls the
candles out one by one and mentions something that
happened during that year of their life. For example,
"When I was three, Eddie was born," while pulling out
the third candle.

Bruce McMullen

For birthdays the birthday person chooses what
they want for dinner and while eating, the rest of the
family takes turns saying one thing they like about the
birthday person, usually going around the table two or
three times.

Kalyn Walker

BIRTHDAY

When it is someone's birthday, they get to choose what to eat for dinner and they eat on the "You Are Special" plate.

Jessie Evans

In my family, whenever anyone had a birthday, he or she would get to go out to breakfast with dad. This was exciting because we got some quality one on one time with him before he went off to work. We never seemed to have a problem with getting up at 7:00 a.m. on our birthdays to get breakfast with our dad. This was a great tradition because it was a time when my dad and I could talk about life and memories. I learned a lot from him during our birthday breakfasts!

Kayte Brown

In my family, one of the best parts about having a birthday is that you get to pick your own birthday song. We still use the words and basic tune of the traditional rendition, but the birthday person chooses the manner in which everyone must sing. We frequently use "Cheerleader," "Operatic," "As-fast-as-possible-with-a-HEY!-at-the-end," and—my personal favorite— "Multicultural," where everyone sings in a foreign language.

Rebecca Williams

On birthdays we have a gift-giving tradition. The birthday kid closes their eyes while the giver of the gift holds the gift above the head of the recipient and repeats these words: "Heavy, heavy hangover thy poor head. If it falls, then _____." It's better if it rhymes—is witty, or has something to do with the gift being given. Then the person receiving the gift has to guess what it is. I asked my parents where this came from and I guess they didn't have time to wrap a present one time and so my dad just told the birthday kid to close their eyes and he made up a rhyme to cover it up. The blank is for whatever the gift-giver can come up with to say. Some examples would be "... If it falls, there will be worms in your bed," or "... if it falls, you might stub your toe," or the slightly morbid "... you might be dead."

Rachel Cannon

Starting at age ten, on our birthday, we go out to a restaurant with our parents. There are eight kids in my family, so this is a special time when we get to be alone with mom and dad and have their complete attention. We get to talk about things. When were young, it was just fun, but it became really special and very important as we got older. We had the chance to talk about college and plans for the future.

Océane Giraud-Carrier

Half birthdays are a big deal in my family. We always celebrate them, but the celebration ranges from a telephone call to a party. My favorite half birthday consisted of a surprise visit from my fiancé, a few telephone calls from family and friends, and a rousing game of ping pong.

Julie Chatfield

Birthdays in our family are a big deal. My mom stays up late the night before our big day and decorates the house with balloons and banners. We get to have anything we want for dinner and our choice for cake. We all usually choose something that she doesn't make often enough. For example, when I lived at home, my dinner was a pot roast.

Andrea Adams

We have a birthday breakfast and PA's (positive affirmations). Everybody takes turns telling why they love the birthday boy or girl or what they admire about them. We get one or two presents. Mom always makes sure to ask what the birthday person would like to have for dinner with the family. Then Mom jazzes it up and always serves a beautiful array of homemade food. She nurtures us through her cooking. You can taste her love in every meal.

Bryan Bennett

Before opening presents we go around and have everyone say one nice thing about the birthday person.

Carson Calderwood

BIRTHDAY

For birthdays, our family has a crystal pedestal cake plate. We don't use this cake plate for anything else but birthdays—all other cakes during the year go on regular plates. As my siblings' children get older and married, this tradition carries on with a gift of a crystal pedestal cake plate.

Jennifer Demma

We always started birthday celebrations first thing in the morning. It was fun to wake the kids up with presents and fun— I always made their favorite dinner and dessert, and they never needed to do chores on their birthday. We also always took a picture of them on their birthday for their Journals. We also include in the journal entry their current interests and a list of the gifts they received.

Patsy Chatwin

I don't know where he got the idea, but when my dad was a kid he loved to mash up his cake with his ice cream so that it was one smooth mixture. He called it "slosh." He taught it to us, and for the longest time we asked for chocolate cake and vanilla ice cream so that we could make slosh on our birthdays. We used to try out different ice cream flavors and dream about opening a slosh store. Slosh is still one of the most delicious things I have ever eaten.

Stephanie Talley

When our kids were growing up, we made birthday cakes in special shapes—a cowboy hat, a care bear, etc.

Steve and Diane Huyett

My older sister's Care Bear birthday cake and my younger brother's pig cake

The one tradition that my father started when my son was little was to give his birthday celebration to my son. When the cake was brought out we would sing to my son and then my father would have my son blow out the candles for him. When it was time to open the presents, instead of my father opening his gifts, he would let my son open them. It was joyful to watch the excitement on my son's face. It keeps the thrill of birthdays alive because after you get to a certain age the thrill is gone. I hope my son continues this tradition with his family someday.

Cathy Haven

BIRTHDAY

Our family has a fun birthday tradition that has been
passed down from great-great-grandparents. If it is your
birthday, not only do you have to cut and serve the cake
and ice cream to everybody, but once you take your first
bite of your dessert you cannot laugh or talk until you
have finished. The guests all try to make the birthday
person laugh by constantly telling them jokes, doing
funny things like dancing and doing tricks. The object is
to try to make the birthday person laugh or talk before
they finish their cake. It gets very fun and serious too.

Cherise Cutter

When I was a boy, my stepmother had grown up with
a birthday tradition that she perpetuated into the next
generation. In addition to candles on the cake, she
had a "growing candle." It was a candle that was larger
than a birthday cake candle, but much smaller than a
standard candle. She had a small brass candlestick that
held that size of candle. It was lit during the birthday
dinner. The idea was that the amount the candle
burned during dinner would be equivalent to the
amount the child would grow in the coming year.

Anonymous

Before opening presents we go around and have
everyone say one nice thing about the birthday person.

Carson Calderwood

My mom is a brilliant cake decorator. She can make a
cake look like anything. The kids would always get
to choose/design a cake and she would make it
precisely how we wanted it (even if it took her all day).

Nancy Jones

When my sister and I were little, it was always a "girly" thing to have a slumber party for your birthday. So, every year we would have one and our unique family tradition was to have waffles with whipped cream and berries on top. Growing up, it was our favorite treat and we still love eating waffles with strictly homemade whipped cream, waffles, and berries. Yum!

Janae Piercy

For birthday presents and other presents, my family has a tradition of giving coupons to each other. These coupons have nice deeds such as washing a car, a back massage, or doing the dishes for someone else written on them. We would give them to each other as gifts and redeem them later on. This was a learning experience, as we loved learning how to serve and care for each other from a young age.

Janae Piercy

My husband makes all the cool birthday cakes that move, sing, light up...he is ever so creative! They go with the birthday theme. Once we had a western theme—the cake was mountains with cowboys and Indians chasing each other around the cake on horses.

Tamra Lybbert

Ideas for your family tradition:

_____

_____

_____

_____

New Year's Eve Traditions

December 31

For New Year's Eve we make confetti by shredding or cutting up colored paper and using hole punchers. At 8:00 p.m. we count down and throw confetti in the living room, throwing it again and again, and then getting into a confetti fight. Everyone scrambles and picks up confetti and throws it. Sometimes they do another coordinated toss. It is fun to try to get as much down each other's shirts, and into each other's hair, as possible.

Lisa Nielson

We write predictions about each other anonymously and then read them aloud. Usually people die or experience life changing events in these predictions.

Benjamin Jensen

We drink sparkling cider on New Year's Eve.

Carson Calderwood

We used to have cheese and chocolate fondue for New Year's Eve.

Whitney Taylor

After the midnight cheering, each of the kids put a pair of shoes out on the porch. Rumor has it that the New Year's Eve Baby comes by and fills them with goodies to bring in the new year. When we wake up on the 1st, we run out to the porch to find our shoes filled with candy, punch balls, slinkies, magazines, and other little things.

Sabrina Huyett

On New Year's Eve my family always makes dipped chocolates. We unwrap a bunch of caramels and dip those in chocolate. We also make peanut butter and coconut centers and dip the balls in chocolate. Everyone has their own fork and we crowd around the double-boiler to dip our chocolates. I look forward to it every year!

Sabrina Huyett

My siblings and me dipping chocolates

When it hits midnight, we bang pots and pans with spoons on the front porch. Dad also gets out his old trumpet and we all yell "Happy New Year!"

Sabrina Huyett

New Year's Eve

On New Year's Eve we always take a BB gun and shoot up the gingerbread houses that we made during the Christmas season. We make gingerbread houses out of real gingerbread and we also decorate gingerbread men to be ourselves.

Laura Nettles

When I have a family, I would like to have a short family devotional on spiritual growth. Then for fun measure everyone's height on a wall in the house.

Charla Aranda

We once had an Ecuadorian exchange student live with us and we borrowed and modified some of her traditions. On New Year's Eve, we all make sure to find some quite time at some point to write down things from the past year that we want to do away with, such as bad habits. Then, as we start to count down, get out a big bowl of grapes. We eat as many, as quickly as we can, because you get to make a wish with each grape. After midnight has passed, we rush outside, taking our do-away lists with us. Then we burn them and sing Auld Lang Syne. It's a good mix of silly and serious.

Rebecca Williams

Every New Year's Eve dinner is completely random. Each family member gets to choose one thing they want to eat and they buy/make enough for everyone to try some. We end up with 8-9 totally random dishes... everything from Jamba Juice, to Wingers sticky fingers, to salad and chili bean dip. It is super good. It is my favorite dinner of the year!

Nathan Harris

New Year's Eve

We have a family party, exchange white elephant gifts, and play lots of board games (usually Mad Gab). My parents also work hard to create an uplifting and edifying environment for people to feel the Lord's love as they are in our home (yes, even for New Year's).

Bryan Bennett

Everyone writes a New Year's resolution on a slip of paper. We mix them up and read them one at a time. Everyone then has to guess which person made which goal.

Rachel Cannon

On New Year's Eve, we have a fondue dinner. Always included are cocktail wieners, cheese fondue and chocolate fondue. We play games and watch movies. We watch the 'ball drop" on television. At midnight, we have Martinelli's Sparkling cider in Mom's goblets and throw leftover curling ribbon from Christmas on the tree, while celebrating with shouts of "Happy New Year".

Megan Baker

On New Year's Eve our kids set out their shoes and the "New Year's Baby" comes and fills their shoes with small treats and toys. We also write down our family goals and individual goals for the new year.

Sally Bender

Ideas for your family tradition:

_____

_____

_____

_____

_____

New Year's Day Traditions

January 1

All while we were growing up my family would hold a progressive dinner on New Year's Day. Each family member would be in charge of one course, setting up the room for the course and having an inspirational thought we'd learned during the year to give during that course. For example, I would be in charge of the appetizer, such as chips and salsa or cheese and crackers. I would get it ready and set up dad's office for us to eat in there. Then when dinner came we would start in the entry way with drinks, move to the office for appetizers, family room for soup/salad, dining room for the main meal and finally the kitchen for the dessert. It was really fun to each take part in making the meal as well as sharing something that we'd learned during the year. I was more excited about New Year's Day than New Year's Eve when we got to stay up late.

Crystal Howarth

In my family, every New Year we tell each other our resolutions.

Daphna Zohar

The Monday after New Years we write thank you cards for the Christmas gifts we received from family and friends. I make the cards, and then each child takes a card, writes a message, and then passes it around for everyone to sign.

Lacey Charlesworth

We always watch the Rose Bowl Parade in Pasadena, CA.

Ruth Hammer

My husband and I take our children for a hike on New Year's Day.

Elizabeth Matheson

My family goes to the beach every New Year's. This is thanks to my dad, who likes to brag to all of his family that still lives in the snow. My dad and brothers get in the water and go boogie boarding.

Andrea Adams

New Year's Day is the day for taking down Christmas decorations. Many are the years I recall carefully placing precious ornaments filled with memories into tissue lined boxes while the spectacle of the Rose Parade played on a nearby television set.

Anonymous

We have a huge family dinner (extended family) on New Year's Day. We have traditional Southern food and always leave a few black-eyed peas on our plate so that we have prosperity in the new year. That's a tradition in the South. Kind of like "saving" for an emergency. Of course you don't actually save the peas.

Tamra Lybbert

Ideas for your family tradition:

_____

_____

_____

_____

Wise Men's Day Traditions

January 5

WISE MEN'S DAY

After Christmas is over and the laud of the New Year has passed, the Judd family anxiously awaits the eve of the wise men.

We do not know what day it was that the wise men in the east finally found the newborn king, but when they did, they brought presents and praise.

Likewise, before going to bed on January 5, we put one of our shoes outside our bedroom door and wait for the wise men to bring gifts in the night

Sometimes this meant a new umbrella to walk to school with, or the one toy that was hoped for, but somehow was forgotten during Christmas.

I have fond memories of Dia de los Reyes or "Wise Men's Day." It is a fun tradition that my mother brought with her from Argentina. I hope to continue this fun tradition with my children one day.

Jonathon Judd

Ideas for your family tradition:

_____

_____

_____

_____

_____

Groundhog Day
Traditions

February 2

GROUNDHOG DAY

On Groundhog Day, we make Pigs-in-a-Blanket and
watch the movie *Groundhog Day* while we eat them
Bruce McMullen

My roommates found a stegosaurus cookie cutter,
which one of my roommates thought looked like a
hedge hog. We figured that a hedge hog is pretty close
to a ground hog, so we made ground hog sugar cookies
for Groundhog Day! My family also watches the
movie *Groundhog Day* sometime during the month of
February to celebrate.

Sabrina Huyett

Ideas for your family tradition:

_____

_____

_____

_____

_____

Presidents Day Traditions

Third Monday in February

Though he was perhaps our greatest president, Abraham Lincoln was a humble man. The flashy and shallow commercialism of the Presidents Day weekend is perhaps an appropriate way to remember our modern sound bite presidents, but seems inappropriate for Lincoln. So each February twelfth, I start the day by reading one of the many deep and thought-provoking writings that came from Lincoln's pen; for example, this selection from "The National Day of Prayer Proclamation of 1863":

"...We have grown in numbers, wealth and power, as no other nation has ever grown. But we have forgotten God. We have forgotten the gracious hand which preserved us in peace, and multiplied and enriched and strengthened us; and we have vainly imagined, in the deceitfulness of our hearts, that all these blessings were produced by some superior wisdom and virtue of our own. Intoxicated with unbroken success, we have become too self-sufficient to feel the necessity of redeeming and preserving grace, too proud to pray to the God that made us!

"It behooves us then, to humble ourselves before the offended Power, to confess our national sins, and to pray for clemency and forgiveness...."

I then pray and ask for forgiveness for all the times I have thought I am self-made, the creator of my own success. And for the remainder of the day, I set aside all the flashy commercial beverages that I so love, and drink only that humble liquid so vital for life: water.

Renée VonBergen

We often take this week to go skiing in Park City with our cousins and to visit family in Utah. Mom always said that we should build log cabins out of tootsie rolls to celebrate President's Day.

Megan Baker

Ideas for your family tradition:

_____

_____

_____

_____

_____

Valentine's Day Traditions

February 14

We are a family of four girls and mom, so dad supplies the chocolate.

Lisa Nielson

Dad buys each child a half-pound heart box of chocolate and buys Mom the two pound giant heart box. Mom buys the kids a different gift each year.

Sabrina Huyett

On Valentine's Day we have a competition for the tackiest outfit and car. The winner gets what they want for dinner.

Linze Struiksma

My dad used to buy all four of us (all daughters) a pair of earrings for Valentine's Day. Then we all wore them to school for the day.

Megan Sorenson

Sometime in the days prior to Valentine's Day we have a tradition to make heart shaped sugar cookies and decorate them. On Valentine's Day morning, I always make heart shaped muffins (I have a heart shaped muffin pan) for breakfast.

Sally Bender

Every Valentine's Day my dad makes a treasure hunt for my mom leading her to her present. Each clue is a different style of poem, all saying "I love you."

Kalyn Walker

For Valentine's Day dinner, I always make a heart-shaped meatloaf. We have some kind of red drink, and afterwards there are always assorted chocolates and heart-shaped desserts.

Lacey Charlesworth

On the dining room table after breakfast, my parents would have each child's favorite candy bar. Most people focus on people with significant others, so it meant a lot to me that my parents remembered us children.

Molly Peters

In our family, we have two valentine's days, because Brazil's Valentine's Day is on June 12th. So we have a tradition of commemorating both Valentine's Days. It is, in a small way, combining the family traditions of two cultures.

Joao Fontoura

My mom always bought me new underwear for Valentine's Day.

Jenna Kimble

We each get one red gift each Valentine's day. I got the cutest red purse this year!

Malorie Lifferth

We have a family breakfast with thoughtful cards from mom and dad. Each child gets a box of chocolates.

Bryan Bennett

On Valentine's Day, the five daughters in our family always had a "secret" Valentine leave a gift at the door and door-bell ditch us. It was usually something like a locket or red sweater—something I'm sure my mother chose. But we could always count on my father. Now, even when we are out of the country, we know that a box of candy will show up via UPS from dad

Jennifer Demma

Every holiday my mother would buy me and all of my brothers matching unders, socks, and ties for the holidays and we would all wear them to school or church or wherever on that given holiday. Green for St. Patrick's, red for Valentine's, flag or striped for 4th of July, etc. It's crazy, but somehow unique and fun.

Jonathan Drysdale

One of our kids' favorite memories is the heart attacks we have done to my husband's vehicle for Valentine's days through the years. It's such a sneaky, fun, surprising and loving activity. You can do this one at other times not just Valentine's!

Gina Woolf

My husband not only brings me thoughtful flowers on Valentine's Day, but has included the children by bringing each of them their own individual flower with a sweet and loving message on the card. Usually it is a carnation and the girls get pink and the boys get blue. Everyone feels so loved, and he enjoys being the gallant hero on this evening.

Susan Whatcott

With six kids in our home, we often will just spend
Valentine's Day at home...but we certainly get our
mileage with their help. We set up "Cupid's Cafe" in
our home and we all dress up formally. (Sometimes
I have prepared the dinner ahead of time, and as the
kids got older they would fix it!!) The kids set up the
"atmosphere" with candles, soft music, and a great
table set up. They will often make "menus" to order
from. They take turns serving us our dinner courses
and learning manners. Sometimes they even have
someone dressed up when we "arrive" to confirm our
reservations and greet us!

Susan Whatcott

Mom always decorated the table for Valentine's Day.
Each person's place would have a special Valentine's gift
just for them. This was a tradition that was started by
Grandma Cook when mom was a little girl. We would
have a Valentine-themed breakfast with things like
heart-shaped pancakes or toast and pink-colored milk.

Megan Baker

When we were in elementary school, Mom made
homemade suckers for us to give away with our
valentines.

Megan Baker

On Valentine's Day, my dad would send my sister
and I roses to school for the special day. It was always
so exciting even though I knew it was coming, just
because we felt special and it made us grateful to have
such as caring dad.

Janae Piercy

We would each draw the name of a family member at the beginning of February. All month leading up to Valentine's Day, we would do service and look for ways to help that person. On Valentine's Day, we made a big cookie with our name on it and left it on the person's bed to reveal who their secret pal had been.

Megan Baker

Mom had a valentine wand with a heart on the end and ribbons coming off of it. If we didn't do Secret Pals, we would pass the wand around instead. How it worked: someone started with the wand and would perform an act of service for a family member. When the service was done, they left the wand in that location. When the person found it, it became their turn to do service for someone else. For example: If you unload the dishwasher for someone, you leave the wand in the dishwasher. When they come to do the chore, they will find it, and turn around to do service for someone else.

Megan Baker

We play "Deal or No Deal" with real money for our grown kids for some holidays like Valentine's etc. Some times they might end up with $50.00, or they might end up with $3.00. It is so funny watching how serious they take it, how they stress over the numbers to pick, etc.

Tamra Lybbert

Every Valentine's Day my mom makes up a little bag of treats and leaves it by our beds so we see it when we wake up. She also decorates heart shaped sugar cookies and gives them to us after dinner. She has taken cake decorating classes so she is a pro; everything she does with frosting is beautiful.

Nancy Jones

In Japan, they have two Valentine's type days. On February 14th is when women buy presents for the men, and then a month later, on March 14th, the men give presents to the women.

Brad Melluish

Ideas for your family tradition:

_____

_____

_____

_____

_____

Mardi Gras Traditions

The season starts on Epiphany (January 6) and ends before Ash Wednesday (46 days before Easter). Celebrations generally occur in February.

My family lived in the South for many years, so every year on Mardi Gras my mom made us jambalaya, gumbo, and a King cake (the traditional Mardi Gras cake). We all dressed in Mardi Gras beads in the traditional Mardi Gras colors—green, gold, and purple. It was tons of fun!

Alyssa Bybee

Ideas for your family tradition:

_____

_____

_____

_____

_____

St. Patrick's Day Traditions

March 17

My mom makes green pancakes and green eggs and ham in shamrock shapes for breakfast.

Brandon Reese

We eat corned beef and cabbage, or sometimes we try out a new Irish recipe. We used to dye some part of my dad's lunch green—like his applesauce—to surprise him. Sometimes we would wake up to find leprechaun gold, or that leprechauns had dyed our popcorn green or given us green popcorn balls, etc.

Cambria Fast

For St. Patrick's Day, we always ate Lucky Charms cereal for breakfast with the pot of gold charm. It was the only time of year we got sugar cereal, and we loved it!

Kristin Mahoney

On St. Patrick's Day, my cousins always have Lucky Charms with food-coloring green milk. For dinner, they have corned beef and cabbage. We just say "Top of the morning to you!" and respond, "And the rest of the day to you!"

Rebecca Williams

I made small Leprechaun foot prints out of green construction paper, and I put them on the stairs leading all the way down into the kitchen and onto the table where the kids find a box of Lucky Charms for breakfast! (I use the same paper footprints every year. I just gather them and save them in a zip lock baggie for the next year!)

Sally Bender

My family has corned beef and cabbage with potatoes for St. Patrick's Day. I have continued this tradition for my family to help celebrate our Irish heritage.

Amber Warren

In our family St. Patrick's day was always one of our favorite holidays. My grandfather came to the U.S. from Ireland when he was twenty-four. Where he was from, St. Patrick's Day was not celebrated like it is here. He loved the celebrations! He thought all of the green and the dying of rivers was hilarious. So, when I was growing up, my mother always made St. Patrick's Day a fun day. My favorite thing to do was dye cream cheese green, and make a sandwich with bread. She would then take a large shamrock cookie cutter and cut out the middle of the sandwich. I will always remember helping my mom make them. Even now for me, St. Patrick's Day is a day I always want to celebrate.

Kerry Mears Perry

Every holiday my Mother would buy me and all of my brothers matching unders, socks, and ties for the holidays, and we would all wear them to school or church or wherever on that given holiday. Green for St. Patrick's, red for Valentine's, flag or striped for 4th of July, etc. Crazy, but somehow unique and fun.

Jonathan Drysdale

My dear friend, Nancy Whitney, always makes green food for St. Patrick's Day—green mashed potatoes— even green milk—Yuck! But her kids, and now grandkids, love it.

Patsy Chatwin

We believe in "Shaun the Leprechaun" who visits during the night before St. Patrick's Day. We got this idea from one of our children's elementary school teachers. When we wake up, a variety of things have turned green! The milk in the fridge is always green, so everyone has cold cereal with the green milk. The kids love it!

Susan Whatcott

My kids make a trap the day before St. Patrick's Day to catch a leprechaun. Somehow every year the "leprechaun" manages to escape! He leaves behind some gold chocolate coins, though, in his struggle to get free. The kids love it!

Sarah DeVore

For the past twenty-two years our family has celebrated St. Patrick's Day by sharing a green meal. We always eat mashed potatoes (made green with food coloring), topped with hamburger gravy, bacon bits, shredded cheese, and mushrooms, green salad, green beans, lime Jello jigglers, and green milk. For dessert, we eat cupcakes made with pistachio pudding and mini-chocolate chips inside and iced with cream cheese frosting with green sprinkles and green M&Ms on top. This has become such a tradition that we mail some of the ingredients to our married children so they can carry it on.

Tim Morrison

St. Patrick's Day

In our family we like to celebrate Saint Patrick's Day and Christmas with green eggs and ham for breakfast. A couple drops of dye in the scrambled eggs, and our kids are giggling like crazy! We read the book before or after breakfast.

Alaina Jensen

The Leprechauns visit our house on St. Patrick's Day. The night before St. Patrick's Day my siblings and I would always decorate a shoe box. We would usually cover it in green paper, put stickers all over it, draw pictures on it, etc. We just made it as festive and green as possible. Then we would leave it out somewhere for the Leprechauns to find it. It the morning we find some sort of trail that the Leprechauns have left. Sometimes it is a maze of green string that we have to follow and sometimes it is trail of clover confetti that we have to follow. We follow the trail and at the end we will find out box that we decorated. The Leprechauns will have filled it up with all kinds of fun treats and gifts for us (chocolate coins, green bouncy balls, green suckers, pistachios etc.)

Nancy Jones

Similar to Valentine's Day, Mom would decorate the table and we would have a green breakfast; which often consisted of "green eggs and ham", shamrock shaped toast or pancakes, and of course, green-colored milk.

My husband's grandfather grew up in Ireland. His family fled there to escape German oppression prior to WWI. Since being married, we have made a traditional Irish dinner every year on St. Patrick's day – including corned beef and cabbage, potato leek soup, Irish soda bread and Irish peas.

Megan Baker

Ideas for your family tradition:

_____

_____

_____

_____

_____

April Fool's Day
Traditions

April 1

We started making a fun dessert dinner for April Fool's Day. We have "birthday cake" for dinner, which is meat loaf frosted in mashed potatoes, and then we eat "hamburgers" for dessert. We make the hamburgers using a cupcake as a bun, a brownie as a patty, colored frosting as ketchup, and sugar cookies for fries. To make the fries I take aluminum foil, fold it like a fan, then pull it out a bit and put sugar cookie dough in the creases, and then bake. The kids love it!

Sarah DeVore

Chayse DeVore excited to eat "dinner"

We do an elaborate April Fool's Day dinner. When we started the tradition, we would turn our seats backward and straddle them to eat, but now we sit normally. A "flower arrangement" is in the middle of the table, which is really just a bowl with flour in it. Dinner is "birthday cake," or meatloaf in the shape of a cake, with mashed potatoes on top as frosting. In our glasses we have blue jello with a few Swedish fish floating in it. Then for dessert we have "hamburgers," with buns made out of Nilla wafers, a mini York peppermint patty for the meat patty, shredded coconut dyed green for lettuce, and frosting dyed red and yellow for ketchup and mustard.

Alan Hurst

We try to pull pranks on each other. One year my older brother put a rubber band around the sprayer on the sink and aimed it so that if you turned on the sink it would spray you. We got him back another year. And I still think of that every time I use the sprayer in my kitchen.

Stephanie Talley

Ideas for your family tradition:

_____

_____

_____

_____

_____

Passover Traditions

Begins on the 15th of Nisan, which ranges from March to April each year.

For Passover, or "Pesach" in Hebrew, we try to complete the entire Seder. After singing the traditional prayers around the kitchen table, we eat food from a Seder plate, which has six positions for six foods: Maror—bitter herbs, representing the bitterness of the slavery in ancient Egypt.

Chazaret—Romaine lettuce that one dips in the herbs to eat.

Charoset—a mixture of cinnamon, chopped nuts, and grated apple, which represents the mortar used to build the houses that the ancient Hebrew lived in (the mixture tastes very sweet).

Z'roa—roasted lamb bone, symbolizing the lamb sacrifice in the Temple of Jerusalem (depending on the family, it may or may not be eaten, since there's not a lot of meat on the bone anyway).

Karpas—Parsley, which is dipped in salt water and eaten, representing the tears of the enslaved Hebrews.

Beitzah—a hard-boiled egg, representing mourning, both for the fallen ancestors in Egypt and the exodus, and for the destruction of the Temple of Jerusalem several hundred years later.

On top of the ingredients on the Seder plate, there's obviously the matzo (unleavened bread) that's eaten, made by the Hebrews for their travels to Canaan (the Holy Land). The reason it's unleavened is that the

Hebrews did not have access to yeast, since it was stored in Egyptian storehouses and restricted to only the Egyptian workers.

However, we always make a special Passover dish called "Fried Matzo," which is exactly what it sounds like: crushed matzo, mixed with some egg, onion, garlic, and then sautéed so the matzo can absorb the moisture and all the flavors. This is not part of the actual ceremonial Seder; it's simply a post-ceremony meal, a take on the matzo served during the Seder (mainly since none of the ceremonial foods act as a full meal, so after the ceremony the family needs to eat something).

Josh Levin

Every spring, my family holds a Passover Seder, also over the phone with my grandparents. My father, having grown up Jewish, recites the Passover stories and songs in Hebrew. As with every Jewish celebration, we cook large amounts of food and invite over as many people as will fit into our house. Instead of doing the traditional four-hour version we do a thirty-minute recitation and a thirty-minute meal

Mike Brodie

Ideas for your family tradition:

_____

_____

_____

_____

Easter Traditions

First Sunday after the full moon
following the vernal equinox

EASTER

We choose our Easter baskets the night before Easter, and Mom hides Easter eggs all over the house. We wake up together and race to see who can find the most eggs. Mom and Dad watch on the couch, having a count of how many there are, and offer clues.

Lisa Nielson

On Easter we would have an egg hunt in the morning and then eat them for breakfast.

Cassie Smith

On Easter, my immediate family takes our Easter eggs to a nearby, steep hill, and we race our eggs by rolling them down the hill. We also have a contest to see whose egg can endure the most trips down the hill. It's pretty weird, but I love it!

Mike Lundberg

My dad takes chocolate eggs, little mini ones, and hides them everywhere—on bookshelves, on candles, inside jars, on top of open doors, etc. and we have to stay in one room while he does this. Then we go crazy trying to get the most. We always divide them evenly afterward though!

Linze Struiksma

My friend's family has a sunrise program each Easter. Her mom would get everyone up before the sun rose. They would have a family Easter devotional, and then eat French toast together to celebrate the Resurrection.

Charla Aranda

The Easter Bunny hides each child's Easter basket somewhere downstairs, and the kids have fun looking for them. For Easter dinner we always have ham and yummy potatoes!

Sally Bender

The Easter bunny is very sloppy you know. He leaves a "bunny trail" of jelly beans outside the kids' doors that leads them in the general vicinity of their hidden basket. My mother explained it to me this way, "The Easter bunny hops around the house, and as he's hopping the jelly beans simply fall out!" For my two kids the Easter bunny leaves a different colored trail for each one.

Anne Tsementzis

One of our family traditions is that Mom makes her special pineapple bars every Easter and Christmas. She gets up pretty early to make them, so they pretty much constitute our breakfast those days. Then of course we sneak as many as we can during the day. (The pineapple bars are basically a pie-crust like pastry on top and bottom, filled with pineapple sauce, then frosted. Delicious!) Another tradition is Mom's crescent rolls, which are also generally made (from scratch) for Christmas, Easter and Thanksgiving. Like the pineapple bars, we are constantly sneaking as many as we can.

Whitney Taylor

Every Easter we have a lamb-shaped cake—it's better if it has coconut on the outside so that it looks like wool.

Rachel Cannon

The Easter bunny leaves clues for the kids to find their Easter baskets. The baskets are filled with candy and dessert baby food—the kids love it!

Lacey Charlesworth

On Easter morning, we have a simple, informal, outdoor church service as we watch the sun rise.

Rebecca Williams

Every year, we got together with my cousins (on my dad's side) on the Fourth of July, the day before Easter, and Christmas Eve. We always had the same meals too, and my grandpa always made his homemade strawberry ice cream. For Easter, the Easter bunny came and hid a small "strawberry" basket of candy out in the backyard while we were all locked in the family room with the blinds closed.

Stacey London

The Easter tradition we had when our boys were little is that they had to find their Easter baskets as well as the eggs. We used a white wax crayon on the eggs and put money amounts on them and if they found that egg they got the cash. It was small amounts like five and ten cents, but back in those days it went further. Maybe the total amount was a dollar. It made the hunting more fun!

Laurie Lynd

For Easter, when we were little, my step mom would make us each a dress.

Lisa Mortenson

Easter

We would color Easter eggs the Monday before Easter.
On Easter Sunday, we would have a special breakfast,
search for our Easter baskets (which were always
hidden), and go on an Easter Egg Hunt for the eggs we
had colored. Mom would buy us matching outfits for
Easter Sunday.

Megan Baker

We have "Creamed Eggs Au Gratin" for breakfast on
Easter morning.

Carson Calderwood

My friend's family has a "Jesus Feast" for Easter dinner
where they eat flat bread, grapes, cheese and other
things Jesus would have eaten. They put a blanket on
the floor and eat on the floor rather than a table.

Nancy Jones

Each Easter, we invite some friends over to our house
and have an Easter party. My dad barbecues and we
chat for a while. Then, we have a normal Easter egg
hunt for all the kids. After that, we set up another
Easter egg hunt that is focused on the Savior. Each
egg has a mini story that goes with the Crucifixion that
we read. I really like this tradition because it helps
us focus on the Savior and how we can improve and
become more like our Him through the power of the
Atonement.

Janae Piercy

In Romania, as in many predominantly Orthodox Christian countries, Easter eggs are traditionally dyed red. I've heard several explanations of this tradition, ranging from a story that there was a basket of eggs at the bottom of Jesus' cross to the pre-Christian celebration of spring, to red being the color of spring. The eggs are hard-boiled and colored red. Then the celebrators are invited to play a game where two people each hold an egg in their hand. The first person says "Hristos a inviat!" (Christ is risen!) and the second replies "Adevarat a inviat!" (Truly He is risen!). Then the first person hits their opponent's egg with her own. Whoever can go the longest without cracking her egg wins! I have heard that this game is also symbolic of Jesus' victory over death, with the cracked egg representing the open tomb. I learned this tradition when I lived in Romania, and I continue doing it here!

Rachel Cannon

Rachel Cannon and Sabrina Huyett playing the Romanian egg game

I make hot cross buns for Easter. I just started this tradition personally this year and I like it! The hot cross buns are slightly sweet buns with cinnamon, spices, raisins/currants, and sometimes candied citrus fruit in them. They have crisscrossed slits in the top where a "cross" is placed. The cross can be made out of pastry, a mixture of water and flour, rice paper, or icing (which I think tastes better). In the UK they are eaten year-round, but they are traditionally an Easter food, more specifically for Good Friday, as the cross on top can symbolize the Crucifixion.

Rachel Cannon

Hot cross buns

For Easter, we have two matching eggs for each of our kids and their spouses. We give them the first egg with a clue, like which room the other egg is hidden in. They then have to find the matching egg with the clue that tells where their Easter basket is. The older you are, the harder your egg is hidden. Examples are, we took a new loaf of bread, in the middle we hollowed out a place for the egg, put it all back, tied it up and you couldn't tell it had ever been open. Another example is, digging out a hole in a decorative candle for the egg, putting the egg in and melting the wax and pouring it back in to cover the hole. We have hidden them in the lawn mower bag...you get the idea. Our kids love it, and are antsy all day to come to our house for the "hunt".

Tamra Lybbert

Ideas for your family tradition:

_____

_____

_____

_____

_____

Earth Day Traditions

April 22

Earth day is a great day to pretend you are a hippie—
wear tie die and cook vegetarian. My family has talked
about doing this, but we have not done it yet.

Nate Carrier

We like to have a picnic on Earth Day when the
weather is nice.

Rebecca Williams

Ideas for your family tradition:

_____

_____

_____

_____

_____

Memorial Day Traditions

Last Monday in May
First established to honor the Union
soldiers in the Civil War

We go on family outings every Memorial Day Weekend. We will see museums, play at parks, go out to eat, read or listen to books in the car, swim in pools, go hiking, etc.

Trevor Bender

Another important Memorial Day Weekend tradition is watching the Indy 500. I have watched it every year since I was a sophomore in high school. Since the drivers are generally the same year after year, my kids have begun to identify with them and choose their favorites to win. In fact we take turns picking a team of three drivers and then see who gets the most points based on the finishing results. And of course we enjoy fun snack food during the race, too.

Trevor Bender

On Memorial Day, Fourth of July, and Labor Day we make homemade ice cream.

Casey Knecht

Every year for Memorial Day weekend, our family, and a bunch of other families would drive seven hours to San Felipe, Baja and just camp out in tents on the beach. This involved off-roading, eating super cheap fish tacos in town, eat at Rockodile Bar & Grill, playing in the sand bars, clam digging, sun-sleeping, eating food out of a cooler, and doing other beach-related stuff. It was awesome. The biggest caravan I remember had about ninety people.

Colleen McGill

My family would go a nearby park that had barbecues and picnic tables, and my dad would make us a pancake breakfast.

Sabrina Huyett

On Memorial Day we go to Torrence to have a barbecue and visit with our great aunt, and we always play Scrabble.

Cambria Fast

On Memorial Day and Veterans Day, we would go to the cemetery and put flags on the graves of veterans. It was a great way to instill patriotism in us little kids.

Kristin Mahoney

Another tradition that we had as a family was going camping every Memorial Day weekend. We would go somewhere close, but it was always fun because we were together. We learned how to start fires, how to set-up a tent, and how to cook outdoors. It was an unconventional holiday that we took to get away and have fun as a family!

Kayte Brown

My family and I began the tradition of camping out with a few other families every Memorial Day weekend. We always tried to get the same camping spots. I have fond memories of year after year getting reacquainted with the same paths in the forest, signing the same fun camp songs, and roasting marshmallows over the fire to make s'mores.

Liz Snyder

For years, our family has always gone to the cemetery on Memorial Day. We visit members of our families buried there and reminisce on their lives. We get to share our favorite memories of them, which is always a treat. After visiting the ten or so members of our family who are buried in the Rose Hills cemetery, we used to go eat at I-HOP but now have changed to making breakfast and eating at either at our grandma's house or our home. We always have an enjoyable time both remembering our family members who have passed on and being together with those still alive.

Hillary Michael

Every Memorial day, my family would go to the local cemetery and look at the graves. There was a veteran's memorial there, and we would read the epitaphs on it.

Julie Chatfield

Our family has the tradition of going away on Memorial Day to make memories together. We don't have any set place we go, so we've tried places nearby us within a few hours' drive...Mt. Rainier, Leavenworth, Seabrook, San Juan Islands, and Whistler. The kids already have school off, so my husband makes the effort to also take some days off. We enjoy going to new places for church on Sunday and meeting new people. We always bring lots of good food, games to play, and get a lot of visiting in while we are away together with no distractions.

Susan Whatcott

MEMORIAL DAY

Most years we had a barbecue or a picnic to celebrate
Memorial Day. After dinner, we would go to a local
cemetery and search for headstones of people who had
served in the military. We would leave flowers at their
graveside.

Megan Baker

Ideas for your family tradition:

_____

_____

_____

_____

_____

Mother's Day
and Father's Day
Traditions

Second Sunday of May and third
Sunday of June

For Mothers' Day and Fathers' Day our parents ask us to make something instead of buying a gift, it can be pretty funny!

Drew Barber

On Mothers' Day the men cook and clean everything. The women do no work!

Benjamin Pacini

On Mothers' Day we kids make mom a special breakfast. Then at night dad helps us to put on dinner.

Sabrina Huyett

On Fathers' Day, Mom makes Dad the dinner of his choice and then we have lemon meringue pie—his favorite—for dessert.

Sabrina Huyett

Each Mother's Day instead of giving presents, we give my mom a letter with our favorite memory with her over the past year. She has kept all of our letters in a binder and says it is the greatest present she has ever received. Anytime she is having a hard day she will go in and randomly open the binder and read a letter and she says without fail it always makes her happy.

Crystal Howarth

On Father's Day we like to decorate Daddy's car so when he comes out of church it is covered with hearts and cute messages.

Alaina Jensen

Even though I'm a mom, I hate Mother's Day! So, we have struck a deal. No one has to buy presents, cards or flowers....but they do have to sing to me. This usually involves a conference call now that they are all grown up. It is a nonsense song we heard Madeline Kahn sing thirty-five years ago and the words are all wrong—but it makes me laugh—hey, I'm easily entertained. It's a takeoff on the song "M is for the many things she gave me." Too funny, but it makes my day. It's a small thing to ask for giving birth, I say!

Patsy Chatwin

We would make breakfast in bed for Mom, although she never stayed in bed long enough. We would make a special dinner for Mom that night. One of my favorite things about Mother's Day is that Dad would coordinate all of the kids to help with the dinner preparation. Mom didn't ever have to lift a finger.

On Father's Day we would make breakfast for Dad and, like Mom, he never quite stayed in bed long enough. We would also have a special dinner, something a little nicer than normal.

Megan Baker

On Mother's Day, my sister and I wake up early and make breakfast in bed for my mom. However, my mom is the lightest sleeper in the world, so we made it a team effort and got Dad involved. We made the breakfast while he tried to distract her from hearing us and kept her from going to the kitchen. Usually, we made pancakes and eggs and brought the food in so we could all eat in bed together to celebrate my mother and how grateful we are for her.

Janae Piercy

Ideas for your family tradition:

_____

_____

_____

_____

_____

Flag Day Traditions

June 14

We celebrate Flag Day by having flags all over the house and having an American dinner.

Nate Carrier

I remember one year that Grandma Leavitt was babysitting us in New Jersey while Mom and Dad were gone. She gathered the few of us together and read us the history of our flag and a patriotic poem. I will always be grateful to Grandma Leavitt for instilling in me a deep sense of patriotism and a love for our country.

Megan Baker

Ideas for your family tradition:

_____

_____

_____

_____

_____

Fourth of July
Traditions

July 4

We used to have a water balloon fight at the Fourth of July. We would spend all morning filling up hundreds or perhaps thousands of water balloons in the front yard, and after fifteen minutes, around 2 o'clock or so, they would all be gone. We would help to pick up the pieces off of the grass, and then eat watermelon with everybody afterward.

Abe O Connor

In addition to the more traditional ways of celebrating the Fourth of July, our family also commemorates that day by viewing the award-winning movie, *Schindler's List*. We are reminded of how freedoms were taken from the Jewish people by the Nazis and of how one man worked to right some of the wrongs he saw being committed. We are moved each time as we see the risks he took to help others, and the suffering of many men, women, and children. At the end of the movie we are all much more appreciative of the freedoms and rights we enjoy, and are inspired by the efforts of one man. Watching *Schindler's List* has become a moving experience for our family on many Independence Days.

Tim Morrison

We usually have a very American meal for dinner, like hamburgers and watermelon and apple pie. Then, of course, we watch fireworks.

Sabrina Huyett

We always go to my parents' house in Oakley, Utah. Watch the parade, go to the JR rodeo and finish the night watching the city's fireworks.

Lacey Charlesworth

For the Fourth of July we take apart all the fireworks that come in the pack and make four or five sweet huge ones that have the fuses tied together in every possible place. It's great fun!

Nate Carrier

When I was little, my dad would take us out on the Fourth of July with another family, and we would have water balloon wars with the water balloon launcher. It was great fun!

Alaina Jensen

My family has had soldiers in the military from before the American Revolution until today, so the Fourth is a pretty important holiday. We make sure that my grandma and both of my grandpas all have flags on their graves for having served in WWII. We have a picnic lunch always with watermelon and lemonade. Then we go to Antietam Battlefield to watch the fireworks show and listen to the Maryland Symphony Orchestra. They play the *William Tell Overture* and have canons accompanying it. We listen to Dad tell stories about the war.

Molly Peters

The Fourth of July was filled with the parade, family fireworks, the city fireworks show, root beer floats, and star gazing.

Bryan Bennett

For the Fourth of July, my family makes a homemade slip'n'slide! It is so much fun.

Malorie Lifferth

We always make waffles and have toppings of fresh strawberries and blueberries with whipped cream...the kids like to use them to make a "flag" on their waffle!
Sally Bender

My cousins and I would usually put together a family float for the city's Fourth of July parade. I remember dressing up for a "Grandma's Feather Bed" float, a Holiday float and a Mother Goose float. We have done a few floats with my children in the same parade.
Lacey Charlesworth

Every year, we got together with my cousins on the Fourth of July, the day before Easter, and Christmas Eve. We always had the same meals, too, and my grandpa always made his homemade strawberry ice cream. For the Fourth of July, we were able to shoot fireworks out in my grandpa's front yard.
Stacey London

Every Fourth of July, we watched the movie *Independence Day* after going up the hill and watching the fireworks around us.
Ariel Bean

Many years, the Fourth of July was spent at Leavitt Family Reunions. We would always have a big pancake breakfast cooked on Grandpa and Uncle Glade's camping stoves. We usually had a patriotic program and would watch fireworks that night.
Megan Baker

We always make homemade ice cream.
Casey Knecht

FOURTH OF JULY

Every holiday my Mother would buy me and all of
my brothers matching unders, socks, and ties for the
holidays and we would all wear them to school or
church or wherever on that given holiday. Green for
St. Patrick's, red for Valentine's, flag or striped for the
Fourth of July, etc. Crazy, but somehow unique and fun.

Jonathan Drysdale

My family has a usual routine for the Fourth of July. In
the afternoon, we gather all our footballs and lawn toys,
and go to the field at Moore Middle School. We set up
the lawn chairs and blankets, eat potato salad and chips,
and play football and frisbee until it gets too dark. At
that point, we sit on the blankets and try to play Uno by
flashlight. All the while, there is a large mixing bowl of
cookie dough with tons of spoons in it, which we would
use to eat cookie dough at will. When the fireworks
actually start, we sit back, relax and enjoy the colors and
lights. When they finish, we fight the traffic to get home.
Once there, we console our dog by giving her hugs and
treats (she gets a little freaked out by all the noise).

Julie Chatfield

My extended family owns a cabin at Bear Lake in Northern Utah/Southern Idaho. Every Fourth of July my mom's side of the family goes up to Bear Lake for a couple of days and have a barbecue and do our own fireworks show. We bring out lots of blankets and jackets to keep warm. It is such a fun place to do it because our cabin is right on the lake so as we sit facing the water watching the fireworks we can see other fireworks going on from the other side of the lake. We always go inside and play games afterwards.

Nancy Jones

We usually attend our church's Fourth of July flag raising and breakfast. Sometimes the kids decorate their bikes with flags and red, white and blue, and ride in the bike parade around the parking lot. We usually relax most of the day. The kids always like me to make a flag cake (white cake with whipped cream for frosting and decorate it like a flag with fresh blueberries and strawberries. Yum! We are allowed to have fireworks here so we usually buy and shoot off our own. Our neighborhood is very brilliant with several neighbors also firing off the fireworks.

Susan Whatcott

Ideas for your family tradition:

_____

_____

_____

Labor Day Traditions

First Monday in September

We make homemade ice cream.

Casey Knecht

We usually take a weekend trip (typically somewhere close by). We enjoy lots of family strolls outside and good discussion time and planning time. We frequently discuss family goals.

Bryan Bennett

We would have a picnic or barbecue to celebrate what was most often the last day of summer. For a lot of years, Dad took us to Denny Creek for a hike to the rock bed waterslides.

Megan Baker

In Spokane, they have a yearly event during Labor Day weekend called "Pig Out in the Park". It is like a fair with a huge variety of restaurants and other food stands. We go every year and rent a bike car. It is like a car that is powered by bikes. We all squeeze into the bike car and ride around Riverfront Park and enjoy the food, scenery, biking and family.

Janae Piercy

Ideas for your family tradition:

_____

_____

_____

_____

Halloween Traditions

October 31

Every fall we enjoy a family trip to look at the beautiful fall colors and go to a pumpkin patch to play and pick out pumpkins. We go out to dinner on the way home!

Sometime during the weeks before Halloween we like to make Halloween shaped sugar cookies and decorate them...the kids love to invite their friends to do this project with us! On Halloween night we always have chili and chips for dinner and the kids invite friends to trick-or-treat with us. After trick or treating everyone comes back to our house and they dump out their candy to sort it and trade it with each other!

Sally Bender

It is tradition in our family that the kids make their own costumes with mom's help. We have a large dress-up box, which helps, but we still have to get pretty creative. For example: shaggy dog by wrapping sister in long strip of elastic and threading long strips of toilet paper through.

Lisa Nielson

We always create a special effect or illusion on our front porch. We have made ghosts and magic talking pumpkins. We create it the day of, for the trick-or-treaters.

Jana

We always go over to the same family friends' house, eat chili and chips, and then go trick or treating with pillowcases.

Sabrina Huyett

My mom always decorates the house for Halloween, and she hands out pencils to the trick-or-treaters instead of candy.

Benjamin Pacini

My mom makes a weird dinner with a menu for Halloween. There are weird words and we do not know what we are really ordering until it arrives. For example, witches brew is soup, goblin fingers is fish sticks, bat wings are chicken wings, and eye balls are grapes. After we order what food we want, she has one of our siblings serve it to us like a waiter.

Brandon Reese

This year we started a new tradition. We set up a table with new toys and other doodads with a number on each item. After the kids are done trick-or-treating they can buy items off the table with their candy (i.e. new Pokémon cards = fifteen pieces of candy). The kids love it and this way they do not eat a ton of candy.

Sarah DeVore

My neighbor does the theme, "The Great Pumpkin" during the month of October. They watch the movie, *It's the Great Pumpkin, Charlie Brown*, and then they do little things like "The Great Pumpkin says" (Simon says) and other activities. At some point on Halloween "The Great Pumpkin" rings the door bell and ditches a little gift for each kid.

Sarah DeVore

My mom would make our Halloween costumes. She also made us a special dinner, which included Pumpkin Brains (macaroni and cheese served in a hollowed out pumpkin), Witches Broomsticks (breadsticks with one end frayed to resemble a broomstick) and other creepy dishes. Today we have expanded to include Mummy Dogs (hotdogs wrapped in breadsticks to resemble mummies) and Blood (or tomato) soup.

Megan Baker

We make homemade doughnuts every year for Halloween.

Darin Humphreys

We have a giant soup party at my house every year on Halloween. We make massive batches of tortilla soup, and all of our friends stop by to have a bowl.

Rachel Connoll

On Halloween we have baked potatoes, chili, and wassail! Afterwards, we have more wassail and a fun, cozy and warm, friend and family-filled home. There is fun music, and we spread our candy all over the floor to trade for our favorites.

Bryan Bennett

We do sort of a reverse trick-or-treat! We dress up in crazy costumes and deliver Halloween goodies to our friends and neighbors. We ring the doorbell and yell "tread-or-trick", hand them the goodies and sprint back to the car and drive away. It is super fun!

Malorie Lifferth

Halloween

My friend's family has a special Halloween dinner.
At or before the dinner they each receive a new funny/
halloweeny/spooky/silly hat. They have to wear their
new hats at dinner. They always have spaghetti, salad,
and bread for dinner but they aren't aloud to use
normal utensils or plates. Some people have bowls as
cups and pans or lids to pans for plates. Some have
tongs for silverware and nothing else. Some even have
mallets or rolling pins instead of silverware. It is easy
to be creative with this activity and it's so fun to watch
other people try to navigate their meals!

Nancy Jones

We make Witch's Brew on Halloween, which is just
homemade root beer with dry ice. We make it in a black
cauldron and the kids and adults love it. Especially as
the night goes on, the root beer becomes all slushy and
yummy! Simple, but fun!

Tamra Lybbert

My mom, without fail, made us our Halloween
costumes growing up. She is an excellent seamstress
and made us costumes from butterflies, to dog clowns,
to bears, to tigers, to Dorothy of the Wizard of Oz, to
just about anything! On Halloween, we eat "Incredible
Edible Ghosts". They are balls of sausage covered by
a blanket of Bisquick biscuit dough with little faces of
ghosts cut out on them. We cook them and they are so
good! We always share with friends and they agree.

Janae Piercy

Ideas for your family tradition:

_____

_____

_____

_____

_____

Veterans Day
Traditions

11 November

Veterans Day

On Memorial Day and Veterans Day, we would go to
the cemetery and put flags on the graves of veterans.
It was a great way to instill patriotism in us little kids,
especially because three of my grandparents were
veterans.

Kristin Mahoney

Ideas for your family tradition:

_____

_____

_____

_____

_____

Thanksgiving
Traditions

Fourth Thursday in November

For Thanksgiving we always gather before dinner (usually as extended family) and everyone tells what they are thankful for and how they have been blessed that year.

Jessica Scott

Thanksgiving is when fudge season begins! Under no circumstances can we make fudge before Thanksgiving. I feel this makes it so much more of a treat. After Thanksgiving dinner, we watch *The Sound of Music*. I'm not sure why, but we do.

India Genack

My husband and I started a Thanksgiving tradition this year. We bought a table cloth, and each year our family will write one thing that they are grateful for with their name and the date so each year we can look back at what we wrote.

Lisa Mortenson

On Thanksgiving we blast the first official Christmas song as we put up the Christmas tree. Also our family passes around a bowl of M&Ms and we each take a few. You say something you are thankful for with each M&M your take. The bowl is left around all day and you must continue listing what you are thankful for with each M&M you take. My mom and I watch the movie *While You Were Sleeping* each year as well.

Linze Struiksma

Our Thanksgiving tradition is the Turkey Butt. During Thanksgiving dinner there is a candle shaped like a turkey that we do not light. Throughout dinner, people turn it this way and that so that the butt is facing someone when they are not paying attention. At the end of dinner, the person who had the butt facing them is remembered for the year as the "Turkey Butt."

Colleen McGill

As our last name is PIErcy, Thanksgiving is all about the pie. Each year, we have about twenty to thirty people at our family Thanksgiving meal. But, we also have a high rate per capita of pie. We usually have at least ten pies. However, my dad has his famous blackberry pie that he only makes one of each year. We always try to convince him to make more, as it is our favorite, but he never does and I kind of like it that way. It becomes a fun tradition to see how sly and sneaky your cousins, aunts and uncles can be! My tactic is to always be the first to snag a piece of pie. We all sit down, I excuse myself and snag a piece before anyone finds out! After that, you see people headed toward the "dessert table" and the rest is history. After eating as much pie as humanly possible, we play sports, play around the world ping pong and watch Mr. Bean re-runs. We always go trap shooting (clay pigeon shooting) before the Thanksgiving meal for fun, as we are all small town kids. It is always an adventure with our family at Thanksgiving time. It is a time to appreciate all the blessings God has given us-even pie!

Janae Piercy

Starting November 1st, we put up a cut out of a tree on a wall. Every night we talk at dinner about what we are thankful for, and then we write it on a leaf and tape the leaf up on the tree.

Sarah DeVore

We have a "Stretch Party" each night for the three days before Thanksgiving. This means that we eat dinner at a family members' house. This is to "stretch" our stomachs in preparation for Thanksgiving dinner.

Lacey Charlesworth

Every Thanksgiving, after we have our feast, we sit down as a family and watch the Purina Dog Show. We choose our favorites, talk about how cute they are, and compare the winner to past doggie champions.

Julie Chatfield

One tradition I love is that on Thanksgiving we go see a movie as a family. Some women stay home with the turkey, and when we get back dinner is all ready!

Stacey London

During Thanksgiving we have two full days of rich aromas while we cook and laugh all together. Many rounds of "I am grateful for... because..." Usually, we have extended family over for dessert and games. Sometimes, we watch a clean, uplifting family film. I love Thanksgiving so much, perhaps most of all!

Bryan Bennett

Thanksgiving is a great time in our family for three "f's": Family, Food, and Football. Another "f" that could be added is Fun because we definitely have plenty of fun eating, playing football, and spending time with family. We always have a good amount of people show up for our Turkey Bowl where teams are divided up, and we play until we cannot play anymore. After showering, we have a large gathering of friends and family at a family member's house and then feast. Various traditions have come and gone at the dinner table, but plenty of food and pies is one tradition that has remained constant. It is always a great time to remember the many wonderful blessings that the Lord has granted us.

Hillary Michael

We talk about the menu together as a family to be sure to include everyone's favorites, and then each person in the family helps to make part of the dinner. As we sit down at the table for our Thanksgiving feast, we go around the table and each person tells one thing he or she is grateful for. We enjoy playing lots of board and card games together as a family on Thanksgiving Day both while the dinner is cooking and afterwards!

Sally Bender

Thanksgiving

For Thanksgiving we make whipping cream, butter, and buttermilk from scratch. We like to play card games as a family, and we make the Black Friday list. We have buttermilk pancakes the day after Thanksgiving.

Carson Calderwood

Every Thanksgiving, and sometimes on Christmas and on other occasions, we make and eat pumpkin ice cream pie, by softening ice cream with pumpkin and pouring it in a graham cracker crust. I guess this started because my mom didn't think she could make a regular pumpkin pie. It stuck and some of my siblings won't even eat any other pie to this day!

Rachel Cannon

On Thanksgiving we had the tradition of getting a new board game as a family present every year. I am sure this was mostly to keep us occupied while dinner was being prepared. It has always been a tradition to spend Thanksgiving with our cousins and, luckily, they usually lived just across the state. As we got older, dad and the uncles would take us to the church to play "socks soccer" on the hard gym floor—another distraction while dinner was being prepared.

Megan Baker

Every year around Thanksgiving time, every family had to bring a bag of stuff they didn't want anymore. It would all be put in a huge pile and then we would play BINGO as a family. You were allowed to use as many BINGO cards as you could manage (I once had 12 going at once and still didn't win...), but they wouldn't slow down for you. Once someone got a BINGO they could go get a "prize" from the pile. Everything that was still left over when everyone was done playing was donated to charity. The point was really to clean out a bit of junk and supply easy prizes for the games. Nobody had to pay for anything.

Kellyn Humphries

Every Thanksgiving, we have a feast with my aunt, uncle, and cousins, and then we pass around the Thankful Tin. Everyone writes on a slip of paper what they are thankful for, and we read them. The Thankful Tin contains what we have written through the years, so it is fun to look back and see what we were thankful for years ago. It puts us in the proper mood to begin our Thanksgiving feast.

Ariel Bean

The women in my family flock over the ads to see which stores to go to the next day. Black Friday is a traditional girls-only shopping trip, as we try to get as much Christmas shopping done as we can!

Sabrina Huyett

Every Thanksgiving, for years now, our family has had a "Dessert Contest". Each family member is asked to create a dessert. The dessert must be completely homemade. Ingredients, tools, cooking methods are all the task of the chef. In the early days, when the kids were young, entries were simple, chocolate mousse, pies, tarts, etc. Since then, we have evolved into quite extravagant entries: ganaches, poached pears, flaming whatnots and Lava Cakes poised in the shape of the Hawaiian Islands! Along with this creative progression, the heat of battle has also gotten intense. I would normally be one of the judges (because of my innate impartiality) along with two other members of the family. But in recent years, I have had to bring in "guest judges" to prevent feelings of bias. Our prizes have ranged from a traditional chef hat, to "The Whiskie" (a whisk attached to a block of wood and painted gold) to simple bragging rights. Judging is always done on Thanksgiving and we rate in three categories: Taste, Creativity, and Overall.

Michelle Lenz

We have a family turkey trot! On Thanksgiving morning we all go on a long run or hike together before we stuff ourselves. We all get "numbers" taped to our backs like we are in a race

Malorie Lifferth

My mom's side of the family always has Thanksgiving on Friday instead of Thursday. My grandma decided to do this so that all of the family could do their own thing on actual Thanksgiving day (whether it be have dinner on their own or with the other side of the family). That way everyone could always be together the day after. This was great for me because it meant that I would often get to have two Thanksgiving dinners in a row! So on Friday we would drive up to our cabin at Bear Lake and every family would be in charge of one part of the dinner. While we wait for all the food to be done we go on a scavenger hunt around the town that my grandma sets up. We all split up into teams with Aunts and Uncles as drivers and my grandma gives everyone a list of things we need to find. We have to go and take a picture of what we found and the first team back wins. She doesn't make it easy either! We come back and watch a slide show of all the pictures. Then we eat!

Nancy Jones

Ideas for your family tradition:

_____

_____

_____

_____

_____

Hanukkah Traditions

Begins on the 25th day of Kislev, which ranges from November to December.

Every December, we celebrate Hanukkah with my
Jewish grandparents over the phone or through gmail.
We light the Menorah, sing Hebrew songs, and play
dreidel until the candles burn out. Each day we open
one more present from our grandparents.

Mike Brodie

For Channukah, my family and I always sing the
traditional two prayers each of the eight nights, we
light the menorah, my mom makes potato latkes, and
we exchange gifts. If we can, we try to bring in other
family members outside of our nuclear one, but not
many live around the area, so it happens once in a
while. Latkes are basically potato pancakes (made
the same way as hashbrowns, but with different
ingredients, like onion, garlic, etc.). They're made
the same way, with oil to brown the outside. The oil,
at least in the Channukah setting, represents the oil
from the menorah in the Temple of Jerusalem that
miraculously lasted eight days during the siege of the
Romans.

Josh Levin

Ideas for your family tradition:

_____

_____

_____

_____

Christmas Season Traditions

Officially starts the day after
Thanksgiving

CHRISTMAS SEASON

In our family, we do the "25 Days of Christmas." We have a little wooden house (like a flat doll house) that has twenty-five little drawers, one for each day of December up until Christmas day. The last Monday of November, we spend FHE writing "holiday cheer" notes to each member of our family. On one side of the note we write something we admire about that person (i.e. I love how dad takes time to play with me when he comes home from work even when he's tired). On the back side we write one thing we will do for them (i.e. make their bed for a week, make their lunch). We stick one "holiday cheer" note in each of the drawers. Each morning from Dec 1 - Dec 25 we open a drawer and read the note then put it on the fridge for everyone to see. It's a fun way to count-down to Christmas!

Malorie Lifferth

We always decorate the house and the tree the weekend after Thanksgiving. We have a fondue dinner that day, and we make Wassail that night.

Carson Calderwood

During the month of December we read a Christmas story every night. My mom has given us a Children's Christmas book every Christmas since we got married and we have a great collection! We also make Christmas shaped sugar cookies and decorate them. We also make a gingerbread house.

Sally Bender

We make candy cane ice cream by breaking up candy canes in mortar and pestle.

Carson Calderwood

As a family, we would choose one person that we felt had truly exemplified a Christ-like spirit and take them a picture of the Savior. We would often write a note on the back letting them know why we chose them. We also always tried to find a way to serve or help a family that may not have been as fortunate as us. I remember buying a ham for a family. When we came out of Church, Dad had left it on the hood of their car. It was so exciting to see! Another year, we bought a Christmas tree for a family whose mother had passed away shortly before Christmas and was not going to have one that year. Another time we did a "Secret Santa" for a family, and left them little gifts on their porch.

Megan Baker

During the month of December in anticipation of Christmas we read a Christmas story every night. My mom has given us a Children's Christmas book every Christmas since we got married and we have a great collection! We also make Christmas shaped Sugar cookies and decorate them. We also make a gingerbread house.

Sally Bender

We have a book of stories that my uncle made that has a story for each day in December until Christmas. Each night we read a story and eat cookies and drink hot chocolate. On Christmas Eve it is the Christmas story.

Rachel

I wrap up all of our Christmas books in wrapping paper and each night one of my kids takes a turn picking out and unwrapping a book for us to read.

Sarah DeVore

My daughter likes to do jig saw puzzles, so she gets a new one from Santa each Christmas. When we get out the Christmas decorations, we also get out the past years' jigsaw puzzles and put them on a card table and work through them during the Christmas season.

Laura Williams

When we were growing up, we would make elaborate gingerbread houses during Thanksgiving break and keep them up as a decoration through December. The table would be filled with bowls of all kinds of candy. We would spend several days making tens of houses that we would give away as gifts. After Christmas we would take a hammer to the houses and eat them.

Lisa Nielson

Every Christmas we hide a pickle ornament in the tree and we all look for it. There is a small pile of "pickle presents" that are small, wrapped gifts. When you find the pickle, you get to pick a pickle present to open, and hide the pickle again. You are only allowed to find the pickle once. We continue playing until all of the pickle presents are gone.

Mike Law

Around Christmas time we always go caroling.

Aimee Ward

A few years ago my mother began a small group called Angel Bakers. In the week leading up to Christmas we bake as many Christmas goodies as we can. Then we get together and put one of each kind into a metal holiday tin and wrap them in cellophane with a bow, and a candy cane. On Christmas Eve day in the afternoon we deliver them to the local homeless shelters to be passed out as a Christmas gift. It is absolutely amazing to be able to help those in need and to perhaps provide a tiny bit of joy at a very difficult time! For some it may be the only gift they receive that Christmas. Also, a number of shelters allow people to sleep on the premises but they must leave in the morning. That means that on Christmas morning like every other they leave for the day, but on that day, we hope they have a little piece of hope knowing that people care.

Anne Tsementzis

Every Christmas we hide a pickle ornament in the tree and we all look for it. There is a small pile of "pickle presents" that are small, wrapped gifts. When you find the pickle, you get to pick a pickle present to open, and hide the pickle again. You are only allowed to find the pickle once. We continue playing until all of the pickle presents are gone.

Mike Law

Each kid gets a Christmas ornament every year and we decorate the tree together, hanging "our" ornaments wherever we want.

Jessie Evans

Gingerbread House Recipe
Lisa Nielson

5 cups sifted flour
1 tsp salt
¼ tsp nutmeg
½ tsp clove
3 tb cinnamon
1 tsp ginger
1 1/8 tsp baking soda
1 c shortening
1 ¼ c sugar
1 egg, well-beaten
1 c light molasses
1/3 c water

One and a half times this recipe makes three houses with no extra. Make two or three days before using it. Keep covered in the refrigerator. Take out two or three hours before you use it.

Sift together 1 c flour, salt, spices, and soda. Cream shortening. Add sugar gradually, beating until light and fluffy. Add egg, then slightly warmed molasses. Stir water into mixture. Stir in sifted flour and spice mixture gradually. Add remaining flour, a cupful at a time, just until dough is soft and moist to the touch of the finger. Chill dough 6 to 8 hours. Remove dough a small amount at a time. Roll out on a lightly floured waxed paper ¼ inch thick. Bake each piece until done (350, 8-10). It may take longer, but bake until as dark as you can get it without burning. It is important to cook it enough. For windows, cut out shapes before, bake 5 minutes, add hard candies, finish cooking.

Roll out dough on floured waxed paper. Cut to pattern. Turn over on greased cooking sheet, bake. While still hot, place pattern on pieces and trim to fit. Let baked pieces cool completely. Decorate before building house.

Icing:
1 lb powdered sugar (almost 4 cups)
3 TB meringue powder or 1 egg
¼ tsp cream of tartar
Water – about ¼ cup

Add together and beat about five minutes. Add water a little at a time so you don't get the icing too thin.

A few years ago my mother began a small group called
Angel Bakers. In the week leading up to Christmas we
bake as many Christmas goodies as we can. Then we get
together and put one of each kind into a metal holiday
tin and wrap them in cellophane with a bow, and a
candy cane. On Christmas Eve day in the afternoon we
deliver them to the local homeless shelters to be passed
out as a Christmas gift. It is absolutely amazing to be
able to help those in need and to perhaps provide a tiny
bit of joy at a very difficult time! For some it may be the
only gift they receive that Christmas. Also, a number
of shelters allow people to sleep on the premises but
they must leave in the morning. That means that on
Christmas morning like every other they leave for the
day, but on that day, we hope they have a little piece of
hope knowing that people care.

Anne Tsementzis

We always read "The Best Christmas Pageant Ever."
My mom reads it to us at night, with the same vocal
inflections every time we read it. We have it just about
memorized now. We also have an advent calendar that
my mom made, of a big cloth Christmas tree, and each
day we pin an ornament on it.

Sabrina Huyett

My friend John has a family tradition where they had
a little manger set up all December and for each nice
thing a family member did, they would add a piece of
straw to the manger so that the baby Jesus would have
a soft bed when he was born. I love that one.

Cassie Smith

Instead of a New Year's Resolution, mom had us write what she called "our gift to the Savior" for the coming year. We would each write ours on a slip of paper and fold it into a porcelain box that sits out all year to remind us of what we are supposed to be working on.

Also, when we were little, mom would put a cradle under the Christmas tree. This cradle was to be for the baby Jesus, and we needed to "prepare" it for Him. When we were caught doing something good, we would get to put a piece of straw into the cradle. The hope was that we would do so many good things that the manger would be soft for baby Jesus' arrival on Christmas Eve.

Megan Baker

Each year we do the Twelve Days of Christmas with a nativity set for another family. Each day we send over one piece (like one of the Wise Men) of a nativity set (bought the year before on clearance) along with a little note about the piece and a small treat or gift.

Lacey Charlesworth

Every year at Christmastime, we would make sure to watch one of our favorite Christmas movies on Sunday evening together. They usually included: *Charlie Brown's Christmas*, *It's a Wonderful Life*, *Miracle on 34th Street*, and now *Elf*.

Stacey London

My family is very musical so we always prepare treats for neighbors and friends and go caroling to their houses to deliver them.

Nancy Jones

I have a friend whose family anonymously provides
the 12 Days for Christmas for another family each year.
Each day leading up to Christmas they leave something
on their doorstep.

Charla Aranda

One of my favorite traditions is every year for
Christmas my mom purchased a new Christmas puzzle.
It was given to us during Thanksgiving Break so that
it would be out on the table to work on during the
Christmas season (and if it was done early, we usually
pulled one out from a previous year).

Stacey London

Every year we spend some quality time in the kitchen
with mom making sugar cookies from scratch. Our
favorite part is decorating them with all the colorful
icing and sprinkles.

Charla Aranda

My mom gives her pre-Christmas life almost entirely
to an enormous Angel Tree project that she runs. She
has helped change so many lives.

Bryan Bennett

My sister made some beautiful, hard cover, spiral
bound notebooks with the title "Recipes" on the outside
and gave them to each sibling and our mother. Every
Christmastime, we send a recipe to all our siblings,
along with an ingredient for that recipe. The cards are
put in the book.

Jennifer Demma

Every winter my whole family gets together for the annual polar bear plunge! One morning we all go to the lake which is surrounded with ice and then stand around looking at the water until someone jumps in. Then we all (or in fact only those brave souls) jump in also. Then they climb out and are covered with the million towels and blankets that we brought and given a cup of hot chocolate to warm up. And someone was of course filming and taking pictures. Sometimes we get our pictures put in the local newspapers since we are getting to be quite a large crowd now! After we get home everyone who jumped gets a t-shirt, they started out in puff paint, then moved to stencils, iron-ons and are now being professionally made with, of course, the year.

Deanne Hansen

In my family, I want to do eggnog drinking games at Christmas time (with non-alcoholic eggnog). We'll play games, and whoever loses has to drink a shot!

Benjamin Pacini

At the beginning of December each of the kids cuts out a Christmas tree from construction paper. They earn stickers all month by doing chores, being well behaved and such, so they can decorate their trees. Then, depending on how many stickers they earn, they receive money to buy presents for each other. I love this activity, because they are working towards and thinking about giving gifts all month long rather than getting them. They love planning gifts for each other and are so excited about wrapping them and watching them being opened.

Carson Calderwood

For Christmas, we have a tree up the canyon we always go and decorate for the animals. We string popcorn and cranberries, we slice oranges so they hang on the tree, and we put peanut-butter and birdseed on pine cones and apple slices. We take hot cocoa to sip on when we are done as we sit in the dark waiting to see what animals will come and partake of our gift. We got the idea years ago from a book I would read to my kids called *The Night Tree*, by Eve Bunting.

Tamra Lybbert

My mom makes sugar cookies in different Christmas shapes during the Christmas season. She cuts them out with a cookie cutter and before she bakes them we all get to paint our own. She mixes egg yokes with different colors of food coloring and we use paint brushes to paint our own cookies. Then she bakes them and we eat them.

Nancy Jones

One of my family's Christmas tradition that I especially enjoy is "The Christmas Book". We read a scripture, sing a song and read a story each night until the night of Christmas Eve where we read the story of Christ's birth and dress up and act out the beloved story. The stories are short stories about love, the Savior, hope and other positive, uplifting Christmasy messages. It is also touching because we all know each other's favorite stories and get excited for them on their days. I have loved getting to remember the spirit of Christmastime and drawing closer to my family and Savior through reading these special stories.

Janae Piercy

At Christmas, when the kids were smaller we had a beautiful handmade, quilted advent calendar that was as big as a door. There were large pockets, one for everyday starting Dec. 1 to Christmas Eve. Every morning the kids would run down the stairs and sit on the bottom stair to hear what was read from decorated Christmas notes. Written on the card would be an event of what we would do on that day. Some of the things we did would be as simple as buying or cutting down the Christmas tree, decorating the house or going out to breakfast. Others would be a special treat like going to see the Nutcracker or a movie at the theater or ice skating. Then some days it was baking cookies for the neighbors, making gingerbread houses, or going shopping for each family member. Sometimes it was a Christmas video that night with popcorn or another treat. Sometimes it was making a Christmas craft. We always had a day to go see Santa and days for the local Christmas parades and or the boat parade in San Diego. Legoland was usually a stop and the lights at Wild Animal Park was a favorite. Then one night we would all pile into the car, including the dog, grab dinner on the go, and traipse through the neighborhood with hot chocolate and blankets to look at the best lights in the city. I still remember watching their faces beam as they discovered what the event of the day was. I still have the advent calendar and hope to hand it down to the kids one day.

Sandy Piperato

CHRISTMAS SEASON

At home in California we go Christmas caroling for
hours every year. We visit at least thirty families every
year. This includes family, friends from church, school
teachers, neighbors and sometimes even a random
house just for fun. We also always bring a small gift to
help spread this Christmas spirit. One of my favorite
parts though is the fact that we all pile in our eleven-
seater van and have fun and chaotic conversations
throughout the two or three evenings we do it on. I also
love the joy we see when we visit older or lonely friends.
Zach Duvall

My family has an awesome way of getting our Christmas
lists to Santa. In our family, we know about the
"specialized elves" called "Brownies". Starting the night
after Thanksgiving, the kids in my family can start
"putting our shoes out." Basically we all grab one of our
shoes and put them right in front of the fireplace where
the Brownies will see them. We put them there at night
and in the morning the brownies will have left us some
kind of fun Christmas treat. We do it about 3 times a
week until Christmas. We put our Christmas lists in
our shoes sometime before Christmas. The Brownies
pick them up and deliver them to Santa. Sometimes the
Brownies even write us letters! This is a highlight of the
Christmas season for me.

Nancy Jones

We also make pumpkin bread during the Christmas season. It is really tasty. My dad will make loaves and loaves of it, and then we give a lot of them away as gifts.

Sabrina Huyett

Grandma Clark's Pumpkin Bread

3 ½ c flour
3 c sugar
2 tsp baking soda
1 ½ tsp salt
1 tsp cinnamon
1 tsp nutmeg
1 c oil
¾ c water
2 c pumpkin
4 eggs
6 oz chocolate chips

Sift dry ingredients, mix oil, water, eggs, and pumpkin; add to dry ingredients, add chocolate chips. Bake in bread pans 350 degrees for forty minutes to an hour.

Ideas for your family tradition:

_____

_____

_____

_____

Christmas Eve
Traditions

December 24

On December 23, we drag out our mattresses in front of the fireplace and have our annual "fireplace party." We read "The Best Christmas Pageant Ever" and all yell the line loudly, "Hey! Unto you a child is born!" We eat snacks, fall asleep in front of the fire, and wake up to Christmas eve. It's great.

Sarah Schultz

Every Christmas Eve our family acts out the Nativity. We dress up as Mary, Joseph, Wise Men, and shepherds, and the narrator reads Luke 2. We have a box of props and costumes that we use every year.

Lisa Nielson

My paternal grandmother is from Norway, so in her honor, we usually celebrate Christmas Eve in the Norwegian way. We make this big rice pudding and it is eaten with fresh raspberry sauce. The host or hostess takes a single almond and scrapes away the outside so that it is completely white, and then they hide it inside the pudding. Everyone is served, and whoever finds the almond in their bowl becomes the king or queen of Christmas! This person gets a crown, some sort of prize (usually made of marzipan), and they get to have their way for the rest of Christmas. It is a fun tradition that we look forward to in my family, and it also helps us connect with our Norwegian culture.

Sierra Wilson

My friend's family has a candlelight dinner on Christmas Eve.

Charla Aranda

On Christmas Eve we do a Progressive Dinner with friends, since we currently don't live close to family. One family makes appetizers and salad and serves it at their house, another house has the main dish and sides and the last house has dessert. We rotate the meal responsibilities every year, and it's really fun! We always start early so we are finished early enough to go home and do our own family Christmas Eve Traditions. Also, this past year the kids started the tradition of a "Sibling Sleepover" in one room upstairs on Christmas Eve.

Sally Bender

On Christmas Eve have each family member give to another family member the one gift that they want to give the most.

Carson Calderwood

We order pizza for an easy dinner, hang stockings, sing and read the Christmas story, open one present— which is always pajamas—and then drive around and look at Christmas lights while wearing our matching pajamas.

Sabrina Huyett

One tradition we have is to have an "ethnic" meal on Christmas Eve. We choose the type of meal/food to eat at Thanksgiving time so that each family can research what to cook (or purchase) for the Christmas Eve potluck.

Michelle Barrios

My American family has a tradition of putting out luminaries on Christmas Eve, from the sidewalk to the door, symbolizing the light of Christ.

Paulo Da Silva

We have a fondue dinner on Christmas Eve. We have one pot with hot oil for cooking small pieces of raw chicken or steak and dipping sauces for them. Then there's a pot with warm cheesy dip for bread and anything else. Later on we do a dessert fondue, which is melted chocolate. And you dip all kinds of sliced fruit, angel food cake, and whatever else would be yummy coated in chocolate.

Charla Aranda

For Christmas, when my sister and I were little, we used to bake sugar cookies with my dad and cut them into shapes on Christmas Eve. We decorated them with those red and green sugar sprinkles and then would each write a letter for Santa and leave them at our dining room table Christmas Eve with milk and the cookies.

Amanda Kidder

On Christmas Eve, my entire extended family on my mom's side has a big party. The highlight of the evening comes after dinner when we gather around the Christmas tree, which sits in the center of the room. My aunt plays Christmas songs on the piano while we join hands, sing, and dance around the Christmas tree, just like the Whos from *How the Grinch Stole Christmas*.

Mike Lundberg

CHRISTMAS EVE

Every year, Christmas Eve Dinner is the formal dinner. We often have many guests because we live far away from our extended family. Dinner usually includes ham, turkey, mashed potatoes, rolls, stuffing, several salads, green beans etc.

Amy Felsted

Every Christmas Eve my family takes a picnic to the San Diego Zoo, and then we come home and watch *The Muppet Christmas Carol*. That night we have a dinner that consists of mostly finger foods and appetizers.

Daniel Tubbs

On Christmas Eve, while we are awaiting dinner, we set up and light our luminaries to put along our sidewalks. It seems to be such a symbolic way to welcome the Savior to our home Christmas Eve. We then enjoy a delicious low-key dinner together. Next, we dress up and perform the story of Luke 2. We use props, and each year we try to do more to make it a spiritual experience. We've added hymns, careful acting, etc. I love this experience. Then, we open a mystery gift. Surprise! Pajamas! We bundle up in our new PJ's, take a tin of Nanna's Christmas cookies, and jump in the car to drive around and quietly look at the luminaries and the Christmas lights. What a peace-filled joy it is to be snuggled up in the car with the people I love the most.

Bryan Bennett

On Christmas Eve we put out milk and cookies for Santa and carrots for the reindeer, and we like to read "The Night before Christmas."

Laura Williams

We have a red and green Christmas Eve dinner. Everything is red or green! And everything is game... green Guacamole chips, definitely red and green jello, red and green tablecloth, red and green dishes, red and green tortelli with red (or white) sauce, red peppermint ice cream, red cherry-flavored soda, you name it!

Holland Denny

On Christmas Eve we make a traditional Italian fish soup called Cioppino. We love our Italian heritage. I think that taking time to remember your heritage and celebrate it is so important.

Kristin Mahoney

I have a friend whose family leaves hay out for the reindeer.

Charla Aranda

Every Christmas Eve, our family does not leave cookies and milk for Santa. Instead, we buy a coconut, break it open and leave the milk and meat for Santa and his reindeer. Of course, we have to test the coconut to make sure it is tasty enough for Santa. This tradition began with our grandmother's parents, but neither of my grandparents remembers the origin of this tradition. Not knowing the origin of the tradition has not stopped us from continuing to keep it alive.

Russell Michael

Every Christmas Eve we have a finger food dinner of
fruit, veggies, lil' smokies, cheese, crackers, cookies,
and hot apple cider or eggnog. After finger-food
madness we all split into two teams and battle for
the year's title of "Name That Tune Champs" with all
Christmas music. It usually becomes ridiculous as we
all try to name the tune in one chord!

Linze Struiksma

I come from a family of twelve kids. We are all grown
now and have children and grandchildren of our own.
Every Christmas Eve we gather at my parents. Days or
a week before Christmas Eve a lot of us get together
and make tamales. We all bring other side dishes for
our dinner. Sometimes there are around sixty to eighty
of us on Christmas Eve. When our kids were little, we
would have them get up in front of the family and sing
Christmas carols solo or with a partner or say what
Christmas meant to them, if they didn't want to sing.
Now that our kids are in their early 30's they don't
want to sing anymore so we have the grandchildren
sing. After a while they are all waiting impatiently to
get their gifts. We have the grandchildren play a game,
like hot potato, and we put music on. They pass the gift
around until the music stops and they get to keep the
gift. Everyone who plays ends up with a gift. We do that
to make the time pass. We used to wait until midnight
to pass the gifts, but now we start around 10 p.m.
Everyone leaves around midnight to their own homes
and have Christmas morning with their own family.

Luz Sauceda

Christmas Eve was always getting dressed up in our Christmas finest then going to Christmas Eve service, dinner at Mimi's, and then reading from the Bible the story of the birth of Jesus followed along with a popup book of *The Night Before Christmas* with the kids sitting in my lap.

Sandy Piperato

We always have a big dinner on Christmas Eve, and we get to open one present, which is always pajamas, and then we listen to *The Forgotten Carols* by Michael Mclean.

Aimee Ward

One Christmas tradition that is uniquely ours is a sock exchange. On Christmas Eve night, we invite some families from our ward and have a party at our house. We always eat enchiladas and play games with all of the people over. Then, the big moment: the sock exchange. The game is just like White Elephant-except for with socks. We go from youngest to oldest and you can have three steals before the socks are yours. Over the years, my mom and I have found some fun other items to put in with the socks, such as Christmas boxers, reindeer ears and some funky socks. It is always a fun rivalry as everyone competes to get the socks they want. One family friend that is close to age in me always steals my socks and would wear them while playing in high school basketball games to rub it in. Needless to say, it is a fun rivalry where we grow closer together and have a great time getting to be with each other.

Janae Piercy

My mom always made a big fancy Christmas Eve dinner, complete with china and linen napkins. I decided to carry on this tradition. I planned months in advance— menu, decorations, favors, place cards, candles, napkin rings—spreading the work out over time made it doable. I made flower arrangements several days in advance and kept them cool in the garage. Any cooking/baking that could be done ahead and frozen made the day go smoothly. I cranked the dinner idea up and usually did five or six courses. It was a great opportunity to teach the kids which fork/spoon/glass to use for what and where it goes. We always dressed up and had a wonderful time. After dinner we had our traditional Christmas program which included the Christmas story out of the scriptures—complete with accompanying hymns and carols, and it even grew to include costumes so we could do our own pageant.

We also have a Christmas box with a reading that reminds us of the meaning of Christmas and what the different symbols of Christmas represent. We also let the kids open one gift—which was always new pajamas so everyone would be presentable the next morning for pictures! Our energy and focus was always on Christmas Eve rather than Christmas morning. There was something magical about being dressed up, reminding ourselves why and eagerly looking forward to the joys of Christmas morning...and it was so nice to pop an apple pie in the oven Christmas morning for breakfast (we got that idea from the Laura Ingalls Wilder books) and then eat left-overs later in the day and take naps!

Patsy Chatwin

CHRISTMAS EVE

Our tradition is that "Sparky the Elf" brings a little gift on Christmas Eve and leaves it outside the bedroom door with a note, written in Elf language. This is to keep the kids happy and busy so mom and dad can get a little sleep after being up most of the night. Sparky always says positive things about you, and encourages you in areas you are working on. Even our older kids still love the "Sparky" tradition. Santa always leaves a note as well that talks about the real meaning of Christmas and how that applies to our lives.

Tamra Lybber

My great-grandma wrote a song that we call "Holly Boughs". Every Christmas Eve after all of the festivities and after we are all in our pajamas, my brothers and sisters and I line up youngest to oldest and put our hands on each other's shoulders (this became an increasingly difficult task as my younger brother David got taller and taller. My hands can only reach so high). We would all walk to our rooms singing the song. The words are "Holly boughs are arching. Bright and green overhead. Children go a-marching to their little beds. Sleeping eyelids drooping, it is growing late. There's no time for stopping. Hark! The clock strikes 8!" We go to bed and wake up in the morning around 8:00 a.m. Once we are all awake we line up again and this time we cover each other's eyes and sing the song again as we walk down to where the presents are. We change the word "drooping" to "waking" when we sing it in the morning. We open our presents and eat blueberry muffin cake for breakfast.

Nancy Jones

After dinner on Christmas Eve, my mom sets the dinner table with all of the kids' favorite foods, which usually tends to be snack foods. They can be eaten any time.

Kendel Christensen

Ideas for your family tradition:

_____

_____

_____

_____

_____

Christmas Day
Traditions

December 25

At my dad's house on Christmas morning we were not allowed out of our rooms until we heard the Hallelujah Chorus playing.

Lisa Mortenson

When it is 6:00 a.m. the kids are allowed to come wake us...they have to sit at the top of the stairs and wait to hear the conch shell blown by my husband as the signal to race down the stairs to find their treasures!

Tamra Lybbert

Christmas morning my dad takes the youngest kid out to check and see if Santa had come and left presents. This was always a fun one because everyone got a chance to be the 'Santa Seeker' and it is still so fun to see the excitement on the face of the youngest when they see the tree with presents under it.

Kalyn Walker

All kids get up and huddle around the parents' door and sing "We Wish You a Merry Christmas" until parents open the door, then we get into bed with them. We have to wait for dad to go turn on the Christmas tree lights and light a fire. Then we line up in the hallway in age order – youngest first, and mom takes a picture. We all take turns with presents. We always have cinnamon rolls for breakfast.

Lisa Nielson

We always eat German pancakes for breakfast on Christmas morning.

Mike Law

CHRISTMAS DAY

The oldest sibling wakes up the other kids at 7 o'clock.
We all go to our parents room, kick them out of bed,
and wait there while Dad makes a fire in the living
room and mom puts cinnamon rolls in the oven.
Then they get us, and we line up in the hallway from
youngest to oldest, and take a picture before running to
our stockings. We all open stockings at the same time,
which all have an orange at the very bottom, but then
we take turns giving out our presents to others. After
presents are all open we eat homemade cinnamon rolls.
Later we have a nice dinner.

Sabrina Huyett

My siblings and I lined up in the hallway one Christmas

Our kids drew names for gifting rather than shopping for every sibling. They also did secret good deeds for the person they picked. As the kids got older these sibling gifts were also opened on Christmas Eve. I loved this! It simplified shopping and wrapping and made the giving more meaningful. As the kids moved away they created a rotating chart so they have someone different every year. When they were struggling students they agreed to make their gifts. The rules change with their circumstances—but they still maintain the tradition and now the grandkids get excited about the tradition. It is so much fun to see these traditions live on.

Patsy Chatwin

We have scones for Christmas morning breakfast with dulce de leche.

Carson Calderwood

In my friend's family they get a Christmas tree ornament in their stockings each year from Santa.

Charla Aranda

For Christmas, we make the "Jesus cake" to celebrate his birthday.

Ariel Bean

We do a hot chocolate bar, which has all different kinds of hot chocolate and things to put in it. It is really fun!

Sarah DeVore

We go to the movies together on Christmas day.

Carson Calderwood

At the bottom of our stockings there is always a scrap of wrapping paper with a poem by dad on it telling us where our last present is. That present is always the big, special one.

Eric Long

On Christmas Day we do not cook. Instead we have all sorts of appetizers and finger foods that we have prepared in the week before. Some of these include homemade beef jerky, crab dip, a relish tray, and a huge cheese platter. Also, we bring out the leftovers from Christmas Eve.

Amy Felsted

On Christmas morning, my kids open their stockings and their gifts from Santa, and then we have breakfast. Christmas Breakfast is always Apple Turnovers and Cinnamon Rolls! Then we open the rest of the gifts, taking turns youngest to oldest. Mom and Dad always give three gifts to the kids: Gold the "Gift of Wonder" (a wanted toy, etc) wrapped in Gold Paper, Frankincense "The Gift of Meaning" (special book, piece of jewelry, heirloom, meaningful gift) wrapped in Red paper, Myrrh "Gift of Usefulness" (new jacket, clothing, something needful/useful) wrapped in green paper. I learned about this tradition from a friend, and we started the tradition in our family several years ago, and it has been a hit. Gift giving becomes more thoughtful and meaningful and helps bring the true meaning of Christmas, in to the excitement of Christmas morning!

Sally Bender

Christmas Day

At Christmas we all give a gift to Christ. We write down what we will do that year to be more Christ-like: serving others, being nicer, etc., and put the papers in a place where we can review them monthly at our family night.

Cassie Smith

One of my favorite traditions growing up was Santa hid all the presents on Christmas day and we all had to wait upstairs until my dad had the video camera ready. When he was ready, we all stormed down the stairs to find all the presents that had been hidden.

Stacey London

For as long as I can remember, my Mom has made pecan logs from scratch for Christmas. As my sisters and I have grown up each of us has carried on the tradition. We make the fondant and caramel, chop pecans and tear wax paper. It's a true tie to our childhood, and it's delicious!

Amber Warren

We always had a huge fare at Thanksgiving so Christmas was finger foods and staying in our pajamas all day. The kids loved the no pressure and time to play with their toys, and I loved the special Costco once a year hors d'oeuvres that we would nibble on.

Sandy Piperato

Dad always gets each kid a tool for Christmas. When the grandsons turn twelve, they start getting tools too.

Steve and Diane Huyett

One year my mom decided she didn't want to get up early on Christmas, so she changed all of the clocks in the house. We all thought we were getting up early, but it was actually several hours later than we thought. The next year we got her back. We changed the clocks so that she thought she was sleeping in but she was actually getting up way early. Every year we still argue about what time we want to get up on Christmas morning.

Stephanie Talley

My husband and I have been married fifty years. Every Christmas morning for most of those years, we have had homemade Cinnamon rolls for breakfast. When our children or grandchildren serve missions for our church, we mail them cinnamon rolls for Christmas morning.

Gretchen Varner

For Christmas my siblings and I have this crazy tradition that started way back when we were little. We come up with this big elaborate plan for how we will wake up mom and dad. We will put on some kind of loud show, sing, blast music, etc. Every year we try to outdo ourselves.

Jessica Scott

We always hide miniature ornaments on the tree and after all the gifts are open, we let the kids, grandkids, and everyone try to find them. They are hidden very well! If you find one, it is worth $10.00. You wouldn't believe how excited our married kids get over $10!

Tamra Lybbert

My mom always seems to have a service-oriented Christmas at home. One that we started a few years ago was a "Service Journal". We ask our parents what they want for Christmas and they always say service. So, each child or family is to write a service journal where we write down services that we have done throughout the year. When we open our presents on Christmas morning, my mom and even my dad tear up reading about the service that we had rendered throughout the year. We really enjoy this as we get to appreciate our family members more and to see the good in each one of them. I also enjoy it because I feel that it helps us remember the true meaning of Christmas.

Janae Piercy

Ideas for your family tradition:

_____

_____

_____

_____

_____

Christmas Traditions From Around the World

In Japan there aren't a lot of Christians, but the whole country still celebrates Christmas to some extent—maybe the same way Americans "celebrate" Cinco de Mayo or Saint Patrick's Day. My favorite tradition is the Japanese Christmas cake. They think they're being very American. In fact, once I was teaching my English class about Christmas traditions from around the world and one of my students asked "What about the Christmas cake? Where does that come from?" I responded, "Um... pretty sure that was you guys." Japanese families buy a cake from a bakery (typically people don't have their own ovens), and they're usually light white sponge cakes with strawberries. They can be decorated with all sorts of Christmas paraphernalia - you see a lot of little "Santa Sans". They eat the cake on Christmas Eve, and sometimes "Santa San" will leave a present for the children while they are asleep, though no Christmas trees or reindeer. Basically, it's a Christmas tradition created out of things they've seen in American movies.

Anneke Majors

*A Japanese Christmas Cake
made by Anneke Majors*

In Spain we eat roasted Lamb as Christmas dinner which is almost like a Passover.

Mario Dealba

On Christmas Eve we have a get-together. We have a late dinner with all of my extended family and wait until midnight, when we have hot cocoa and Panetón (a sweet, fluffy fruitcake). Then all of our family exchanges presents and we don't go home until two or three in the morning. That's what we used to do in Peru, so we still do it.

Janet Call

During holidays and especially during Christmas, Mexicans from northern states love making tamales in huge batches. The whole Christmas season smells like steaming tamales drifting across the breeze. Most tamales are made of thick cornmeal with a filling of stringed chicken, beef, or pork. They wrap each tamale in a corn husk and pressure-cook them in enormous metal pots. No one is shy about the quality of their wife's tamales, and it's impossible for visitors to escape without being offered a large bag bursting with hot tamales.

Matt Bird

I am from France, and throughout the month of December my family gathers around the nativity scene, and we light a sparkler on the hay roof.

Clémence Destribois

In Romania, children go Christmas caroling to friends'
and neighbors' homes. The carolers receive anything
from coins to cozonac (a sweet bread similar to
fruitcake or cinnamon bread) with carbonated juice to
a full-course meal.

Rachel Cannon

In my family we always go over the story of the nativity
on Christmas Eve. As a general rule, in France, people
feast on Christmas Eve—it's like Thanksgiving dinner
here, but with even more food! We start eating late,
and as usual, take hours to eat. There are six or more
different courses: escargots, frog legs, foie gras, rabbit,
duck, oysters, salmon...and it goes on and on. Turkey
is pretty common for Christmas day dinner, usually
prepared with chestnuts. Other than that, instead
of stockings, it's usually shoes. People usually go to
Catholic mass for Christmas and Easter; it is kind of
a big deal. Christmas is also a family holiday, with
grandparents, uncles, aunts, everyone. The most
important things I would say are food and family for
Christmas in France.

Océane Giraud-Carrier

In Russia, we celebrate Christmas on January 7th. It
is a small holiday, spent with family. New Year's is
much bigger; that's when we get presents. We don't do
presents for Christmas.

Anya Golotina

In France they make a Buche de Noël, or Yule Log, to celebrate Christmas. This is an elaborate cake made to look like a log. They'll put mushrooms on them made out of frosting or marzipan, to look more real. Sometimes they are made with ice cream. You can also put berries with marzipan-leaf clusters on it. I also ate it in Switzerland; it is a tradition in most of the French-speaking world. This originated from a tradition in which the father of the house would put a big log on the hearth on Christmas Eve and burn it on Christmas Day. As people moved into apartments and smaller houses, fireplaces were replaced with cast-iron stoves, so the tradition changed, and fathers would put a small log on the table. At some point, this small log was replaced with cake in the form of a log.

Spencer Greenhalgh

The Marché de Noël, or Christmas Market, is a big tradition in France. Vendors set up little booths selling everything associated with Christmas in France—nutcrackers, ornaments, mulled wine, waffles, chestnuts, a dozen different kinds of nativities, and more. It is usually in an old part of town in an open area, and there are strings of lights illuminating the night. It is always crowded, and it is fun to go around and look at everything.

Spencer Greenhalgh

Christmas Traditions
From Around the
World

December 6th is when the Christmas season really
starts in Germany. The children place their shoes
in front of their door, and Nikolaus (St. Nicholas)
comes and places candy in their shoes. He also has a
servant (Knecht Ruprecht or Krampus depending on
the region) that will beat unruly children, who usually
comes with Nikolaus when he makes house calls.

Every family has a Christmas wreath that is usually set
on a table, and it has four candles on top. On the Sunday
with only four weeks left until Christmas, a single candle
is lit, with the family usually singing Christmas songs
together. The next week the same thing happens, except
two candles are lit instead of one. This repeats until all
four candles are lit.

On Christmas Eve one parent (or grandparent) usually
takes the children on a walk to one of the famous
Christmas Markets, sometimes called the "Christ Child
Market." While the family is out, the adults that were
left behind prepare the presents, cookies, and other
Christmas goodies for the children to discover once the
trip to the "Christkindlmarkt" is over. When the children
return the parent that was left behind exclaims, "Guess
who came while you were gone! The Christ Child!" The
children are then allowed to open presents and feast on
the Christmas goodies that were set out for them.

Richard Morris

In Provence, France, they have the tradition of the thirteen desserts of Christmas. They represent Jesus and the twelve apostles. People set out these desserts on Christmas Eve and leave them December 27. The exact desserts vary, but there are always thirteen. They usually include dried fruits, nuts, fresh fruit, and sweets.

Spencer Greenhalgh

Ideas for your family tradition:

_____

_____

_____

_____

_____

Post-Christmas
Traditions

December 26 and beyond

After Christmas we save our Christmas tree outside until it dries out, then we burn it in our fire pit. The flames go really high! It is even more fun when we gather more trees and make a gigantic fire. This probably only works where it doesn't snow.

Sabrina Huyett

After Christmas we gather up a bunch of Christmas trees and I spray them with water and make an ice castle play structure for my kids. We gather anywhere from ten to forty-five trees from the neighbors. I take the fabric part off of the trampoline and secure the tree trunks to the metal rim. I put the misting attachment onto the hose, and leave it on all night to spray the trees. After three really cold nights (it needs to be 15 degrees or below), the trees get so hard that even I can climb on them! Then I place a pallet in the center, to make the base for a cave, and I pile more trees on top. If it's cold, it'll stay all winter, and all the neighbor kids love to play on it.

Kevin Rawle

Ideas for your family tradition:

_____

_____

_____

_____

_____

Neighbor Gift
Traditions

Being neighborly

I always get something for my neighbors for Christmas. One year I filled the middle of wire whisks with Hershey's kisses and wrapped it in cellophane with a note saying, "We Whisk You a Merry Christmas!"
Sarah DeVore

During October someone starts anonymous treat-giving in the neighborhood by making a treat and attaching a paper ghost with the word "Boo!" on it. They leave it on the doorstep of a few houses with instructions saying "You've been 'boo'd'! Make two copies of the ghost paper and boo two other families."
Sarah DeVore

Ideas for your family tradition:

_____

_____

_____

_____

_____

_____

School Traditions

When our report cards arrive we always "go out for good grades," which means that we go get ice cream together to celebrate everyone's good grades.

Sabrina Huyett

While growing up, all of us Taylor kids were involved in various extracurricular pursuits, including theater, choir, band, orchestra and the like (we were very artsy-nerdy and not at all athletic...). The tradition was that whenever someone had a concert or a play, we got donuts that night.

Whitney Taylor

Whenever we had a Monday off from school as a family we usually did something together (my dad was usually able to take the day off from work as well). Some favorites were: going out to breakfast, going to see a movie, or going to the beach, or going to the park to play tennis together (which none of us were ever very good at it, so it was pretty entertaining)

Stacey London

We take pictures of school projects and then instead of saving the projects to collect dust, we have a big bon fire and burn them. We loved it! Burning my physics project was a highlight of my high school career—I had several friends over, and my dad, a chemistry teacher, brought home spray bottles of chemicals to make the fires different colors—it was awesome!

Sabrina Huyett

On the morning of the first day of school, mom made a special breakfast. When we were in elementary school, she would follow the bus to school and be there to take our picture when we got off the bus. She often sent us to school with a special memento from home so that we wouldn't miss our family while we were gone. Mine was always pennies – one for each member of my family. Then, if I felt nervous or alone, I could stick my hand in my pocket and feel the pennies and know that Mom was thinking about me too. As we got older, Mom would write us a note and leave it on our bed along with our favorite candy bar for when we came home from school.

Megan Baker

On holidays, Mom would pack our lunches especially for that day. We would have a holiday-themed-napkin, a special note, and related food. On Valentine's Day we would get a pink cupcake, etc.

Megan Baker

My favorite memories as a kid coming home from school each day was looking forward to reading stories with my mom. We would sit in the corner in our favorite rocking chair in the corner and read good books together. I love this tradition and want to continue it in my future family, as we grew closer together and my mom instilled in me a love of learning and reading.

Janae Piercy

In Germany, on the first day of school in first grade, all students receive a Schultüte (School Cone). They come in different shapes, colors, and sizes. The parents fill it up with candy and school supplies or other fun items: pencils, crayons, coloring books, erasers, fun pens, etc. The cone can come in one of three ways: parents can buy a pre-filled cone at the store, parents can buy an empty cone and fill it themselves, or the children can make the cone in Kindergarten at the end of the year. In my kindergarten there was a dinosaur theme that year for cone-making, so we chose colors for the body, spots, scales, and spikes. The parents give the kid the cone the morning of the first day of school. You're happy and excited—yay, school is a happy place. Then

off to school you go, with your cone (there is tissue paper to cover up what's inside). The school authorities talk to everyone, and the kids to go class for an hour to meet the teacher and their class. Then they take class photos and individual photos, with the cone of course. Then the parents pick you up and back home you go. What a great first day of school!

Kimberly Webb

Kimberly Webb with her Schultüte

147

Ideas for your family tradition:

_____

_____

_____

_____

_____

Vacation Traditions

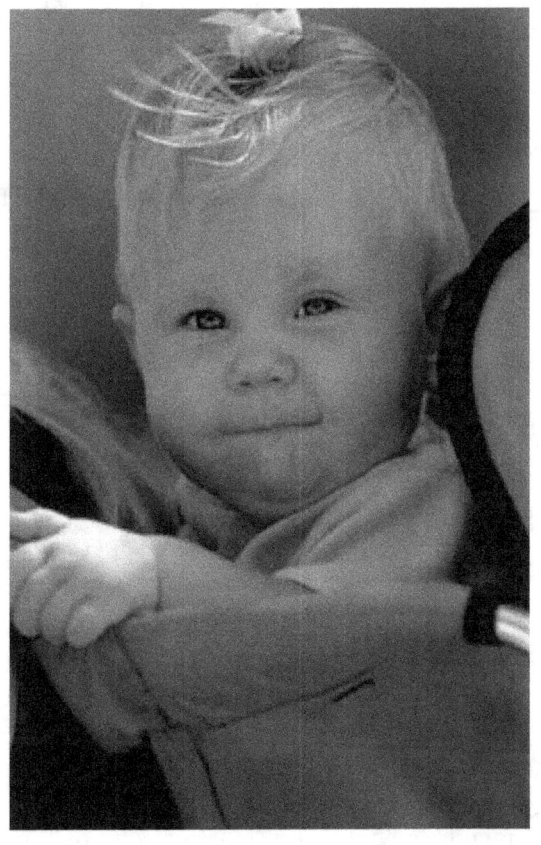

My family often steals away on weekend camping trips. We go to the desert, mountains, and sometimes the beach. We hike, eat Dinty Moore stew for dinner and pancakes for breakfast, and play lots of card games. My favorite part is that as we fall asleep in our trailer, dad often makes up stories. The story continues for as many nights as the camping trip. I also recall dad teaching us a lot during these camping trips. We learned about various plants and animals, and at night he would point out different constellations.

Sabrina Huyett

Whenever we have a long car drive associated with a family vacation, we buy sugar wafers to eat in the car. It is the only time we eat that kind of cookie, so it makes it special!

Sabrina Huyett

We drive everywhere from our home in Washington, D.C., especially to Ohio and Georgia, where we go about twice a year. Sometimes we go on a whim to wherever. The only questions are, "how long is our weekend, and how far can we drive?" We kids do whatever we can get away with in the car (meaning pranks and jokes) when Mom and Dad are in the front seat. When my brother drove, we couldn't really get away with anything. Whenever we go to Ohio, it's always the same thing: we always go to the Dairy Farm and miniature golfing. We also flatten coins on the railroad tracks and we race homemade boats down Mud Creak. It's really fun.

Missy Bethke

On our long car drives to visit our grandparents every summer, we would entertain ourselves by playing a variety of what we call "car games" as well as signing our favorite travel songs. Our favorites include the alphabet game (each player silently tries to find each letter in the alphabet in order by looking at passing billboards, signs, and license plates), twenty questions, the name game, ghost, and the list could go on and on!

Liz Snyder

When I was little, we used to go on a lot of road trips, so we invented a lot of games to play while driving. One was to play the alphabet game, but since we were from a rural area, it didn't hold our attention for very long. My mom would always listen to the same CDs. Because of this, we all still have the words to "Copa Cabana" memorized and can sing just about any Michael McLean song you can imagine. We also used to do a story-telling game. We would start with the youngest and have them start a story, and then each family member would add on. We would add on and put our own unique individual spin on it until we got bored. My mom said that going on road trips was a cheap way for us to be together and explore when I was little, so her and dad would randomly decide on a Saturday to go on a road trip, pack rolls and peanut butter and all jump in the car and go for a spin. It was a fun way for us to all be together and have fun.

Janae Piercy

We go on a family vacation every other year

Aimee Ward

I loved outings with my family when I was a child. We didn't necessarily do the same thing annually, but enjoyed a variety of fun day trips and longer trips. Sometimes in the fall we went pine nut hunting. Sometimes in the winter we went to the mountains to go play in the snow. One time in the spring we went to Lancaster to see the poppies in bloom. Another time we went to Joshua Tree in the spring. Dad often took us camping in the summer. Rock Creek, Twin Lakes, Zion, Bishop, Sequoia and more. We took a few big trips too, Yellowstone, Hawaii, St. Louis, and Nauvoo. We often visited my older brothers and sister in their homes, and had a few visits with great aunts and uncles. I asked my dad once why we didn't have a summer house somewhere. He said, "because then we'd have to go to that one place all the time." I'm glad I got to go many places as a child and build many memories with my family.

Elizabeth Matheson

Whenever we are driving anywhere for a vacation, we always have meatloaf sandwiches that my wife makes. We feel connected and well cared for when we are all eating our sandwich.

Dave Hammer

Every year my mom would save loose change, and collect it in a 5-gallon glass water jug. This jug was our "Schlitterbahn Fund" and every summer Mom used the money to pay for a family vacation to Schlitterbahn (a huge water park outside of San Antonio).

Amy Felsted

In my family we had a big glass jar in my parents' room that we all put our spare change in whenever we had any or found any. When it finally added up to a significant amount, we decided where we wanted to go on vacation (usually it was Disneyland). It taught us delayed gratification and was more fun because we watched our little coins add up to getting us to a vacation.

Lisa Hatch

When I was really little, my dad's family would all rent a cabin and go skiing for a weekend. There are twenty cousins on that side, and we would rent one cabin and all of us would pile in and stay there and ski during the day. It was fun because we all got to be together, we love skiing and it was definitely an experience having twenty people in a cabin!

Janae Piercy

Ideas for your family tradition:

_____

_____

_____

_____

_____

Family Reunion Traditions

Getting the whole family together

FAMILY REUNION

Since 1956, there is a Michael Family Reunion held in Ferry County, Washington. The tradition began when our grandfather's grandmother lay on her deathbed in the hospital. The family gathered at her bedside and afterward went to the city park to have a picnic. Fifty-four years later, the family still gathers, representing the sixth generation of the tradition.

Hillary Michael

At least once a year all my extended family gets together to have a kind of family reunion. We go to a restaurant and have lunch or dinner, then afterward we all sing songs that we have made up as a family and songs that my grandma use to sing. They are really funny, loud songs, and every time we get together we sing the same six or seven songs!

Joaquin Fenollar

My extended family is so spread out that we only get together for a few days once every two years. To make up for time apart, we celebrate one holiday per meal (with the exception of Christmas, which gets a whole day). For example, at lunch we might have spaghetti for Columbus Day and then celebrate the 4th of July with hot dogs and fireworks for dinner.

Rebecca Williams

I have three "sides" to my family, and each of them has a different way of doing family reunions. The Huyett side gets together whenever we happen to all be in town. The Hammer side has a reunion every other year, which usually entails going to a park, having a barbecue, and playing games. Grandpa usually makes homemade ice cream, which is super tasty. Sometimes we go camping or rent a big cabin. The Clark side has reunions every year. I have fond memories of all of us getting rooms at the same hotel and playing for hours in the pool. Once we all went to Disneyland. No matter where we are, Grandma's room is always the rendezvous spot, as she always has quite a stash of candy. I really appreciate the effort my grandparents put into planning these reunions. It was fun to play with my cousins, and without the reunions I am not sure I would get to know them.

Sabrina Huyett

Every year we have a family reunion, and each family performs a skit about the events of the past year.

Kendel Christensen

Ideas for your family tradition:

_____

_____

_____

_____

_____

Parent-Child Bonding Traditions

When I was growing up, I got to have a "night out" with either mom or dad every three months. It would have been a lot more often, but there were six kids in my family and two "nights out" a month was as much as my parents could handle. In January I would go with my mom, then in April I would go with my dad, and so forth. What we did was up to me. We could go to an activity or out to dinner, and then there was always dessert afterwards. We would spend the night talking about what I was up to and doing something I thought was fun. Once I went to my first horror movie with my mom, and another time I convinced my dad to take me to a Star Wars convention. Not every night out was lavish, but every one of them represented the care that my parents had for me and my siblings.

Spencer Greenhalgh

My Dad and I always went on walks on Sundays after church. It was a great time to talk away from the hustle and bustle of our house.

Kristin Mahoney

Dad takes each of us kids out on individual weekend backpacking trips. It's a really good bonding experience.

Sabrina Huyett

Mom wrote a parody of a song for each child and sang it to them when they were little.

Drew Barber

I have been impressed when visiting my son's family.
They have five kids, and each of their children has one
night during the week to stay up later than the other
kids. They choose how to spend their special time with
Mom and Dad—playing a game, reading, cooking, etc.
The activities the kids choose are quite varied and
creative! The other kids cooperate with going to bed on
time or they lose their night that week. Genius!

Susan Whetten

I grew up with three siblings. So, once a month, three
times a year, it was our turn to have a date with one of
our parents. For example, my turn was in March with
my mom, and then my next turn was July with my dad,
and the next was November with my mom. We were able
to go out to eat wherever we wanted to (within reason of
course). Whenever I went with my dad, we always went
to Coldstone. I loved being able to have that one-on-one
time with one of my parents a couple of times a year. It
was a lot of fun and being away from home, I miss it.

Stacey London

Another one of my favorite traditions was on the first
Sunday of the month, my dad would spend maybe
ten minutes and sit down with each of us in the living
room and just ask us how we were doing—how school
was going and if we had any concerns. We would share
stories and laugh together. It helped me get closer to
my dad, which could be difficult sometimes because
he worked full-time and when he was at home, he was
on the computer doing work or some other project he
needed to do.

Stacey London

About once a quarter (there were seven kids, so it was too hard to do once a month), my mother would call her children each individually into her bedroom and we'd sit on her bed having an M&M interview. M&M stood for "Mom & me" and there was a big bag of M&Ms there to share. We discussed our goals, how we were doing on goals we had set in scouting or youth group, our relationship with siblings, anything we'd like to see changed, ideas for family vacations, etc. She made sure we had plenty of M&Ms to take with us when the interview was over.

Jennifer Demma

We would do "Daddy Dates" while my children were growing up. Once a week one child would pull a date idea out of a jar (all ideas were prescreened by dad) and they would get to spend alone time with their father. This could be a walk, ice cream, or game time, I'm too old to remember all of the ideas, but I do remember how the kids looked forward to their "date".

Patsy Chatwin

Every holiday I would arrive home to find a "happy day" card left on my pillow from my mom. It was usually a large index card without lines on it with one side decorated and written "HAPPY DAY," and the other side would tell what a great son I was and why she was so glad that I was part of her family and thanking me for being so wonderful. Occasionally she'd put one on our pillows when she knew we were having a hard week, or if she was having a hard week. It wasn't every holiday, but it was a lot of them. I never thought about keeping the notes, but I always thought it was way cool.

Jonathan Drysdale

Parent-Child Bonding

Every Sunday I would put on my pajamas and crawl into my parents' big comfy bed for special time with my dad. Sometimes I would get to pick the book and other times my dad would, but we would take turns reading a book and scratching each other's backs. We would also just talk about my week and my thoughts. Then my dad would fall asleep and I would crawl out of bed without waking him and go off to my playing. It was not until years later that I found out the whole reason for that was to have me take a nap, but my mother would walk in to find me playing and my dad taking a nap... it must have seemed a bit backwards to her.

Kellyn Humphries

After the birth of one of our children we were having difficulties with one of the siblings adjusting to the new family dynamic. We decided to implement a special date day. Each Saturday one of the children gets to pick if they want to go on a date with mom or dad. It is usually only about one to two hours long, but for that time they have our undivided attention and it is one-on-one time. We rotate kids each week and it has become something they really look forward to and cherish. It can be such a simple thing, like riding bikes or going to the park. We usually give them a few options to choose from and they really love it.

Paige Guymon

My mom wrote a song for each of us when we were born that she sings to us as a lullaby

Kendra Hammer

On Take Your Daughter to Work Day each year, my dad would invite me to come to work with him. My mom and I would dress me up with suspenders, a dress shirt, and pants to like my dad, Chief Holloway. Throughout the day, his coworkers would send me on little errands and call me Chief Holloway. My mom and dad also made it a point for us to go out to lunch together on "our" lunch break and enjoy our time together. Whenever we visited my dad at work, my sister, Mom, and I would write "love notes" on the whiteboard in his office to brighten his day. I really liked this tradition of going to work with my dad because I look up to my dad a lot and I enjoy spending time with and learning from him.

Janae Piercy

My dad takes a different child out to breakfast each Saturday. It is good one-on-one bonding time with dad. We take turns by birth order.

Maria Dickson

Ideas for your family tradition:

_____

_____

_____

_____

_____

Grandparent-Grandchild Bonding Traditions

My favorite tradition ever is called "Grandma's Camp." Every summer since I was about eight years old all of my cousins who were about the same age as me on one side of my family and I would get together at my grandparents' house for a week for what was called "Grandma's camp". We would do different things every day such as: ride the train to LA and go to a museum, drive to a beautiful garden, learn how to make food from different countries, go to the library and learn how to research, go to the beach, or a friend's house and learn how to quilt. Anything and everything was an option as long as it was not too far away and did not cost too much money. Then one night my grandma always went to the family history center and so my grandpa would put on his old fishing vest and we would fill all the pockets with treats and drinks and go to the movies! But my grandma always said the most important part was taking pictures of everything we did and writing about it. Every night we would tell her what we did and she would type it up, print off a copy for each of us which we would then decorate and put into a small binder. At the end of the week we would get our pictures developed, glue them onto colored paper and intersperse them throughout our binders. I now have a thin binder of all my grandma's camps and love looking back through them. It was truly a great time for me to draw closer to not only my grandparents but also all of my cousins, some of whom I did not get to visit that often. I hope to continue the tradition when I have my own grandchildren.

Kellyn Humphries

We do a "princess shopping trip" with Grandma. Every summer, Grandma takes her granddaughters shopping and buys them one item for school.

Malorie Lifferth

For my whole college career, I went to my grandma's house for Sunday dinner every week. As many cousins, siblings, uncles and aunts as we could muster would come and enjoy Grandma's home cooked meals, usually consisting of a roast and potatoes. Sometimes we would be assigned something to bring (i.e. dessert, a side, a drink). My grandma would make these assignments, as well as organize carpools, by a mid-week email. For an eighty-year-old woman, she was very proficient at emailing. When dinner was over, the crowed would clean the dishes, take the extra leaves out of the table, put away the extra chairs, and things would usually deteriorate into a game of Uno.

Julie Chatfield

My grandmother recognized the birth of every great grandchild by knitting a small baby afghan of either pastel pink or pastel blue using ultra soft baby yarn. We have been able to pass these heirlooms onto our children when they became parents.

Anonymous

We visited my dad's parents regularly, and each time we left, Grandpa gave each of us a package of Peanut M&Ms to eat on the way home. He would remind our parents to take good care of us, telling them to "Hug 'em tight."

Ariel Bean

My grandma always has "Grandma's Workshop" a few days before Christmas where all of the grandkids twelve and under go over and make Christmas goodies with Grandma (like chocolate covered cashews....mmm).

Nancy Jones

Ideas for your family tradition:

_____

_____

_____

_____

_____

Spiritual Traditions

Every night we have family prayer, and afterward we all place one of our hands together in the middle in football-huddle fashion and chant our family cheer, which goes, "Do the Michaels choose the right? Yes we do with all our might. Goooooo Michaels."

Russell Michael

Once a week my family has a "Family Night." We sing and pray, talk about things that are important to us, have a fun activity, and take care of family business. I really valued this growing up, and I am doing it now in my family.

Jared Hulme

We have a winter holiday tradition that worked well with the children as they were getting older and paying closer attention to their scripture reading. We would spend one hour in the mornings and one hour in the evenings on the weekends and on the days everyone was out of school listening to and reading the scriptures. We often could complete the whole book of scripture over the holiday.

Susan Schow

It's a rule in my family that you can't go to bed before we say family prayers. Whenever someone is tired enough to want to go to bed (usually Dad), we gather in the living room and kneel. Our family is really playful, so it usually takes a few minutes for us to settle down to a reverent enough state. A different family member says the prayer each night.

Julie Chatfield

Foundational traditions for us have to include: family
scripture study, family prayer, church attendance,
temple attendance, baptisms, singing hymns,
church activities, and service. Talk about faith
being foundational to identity! Also, learning and
memorizing scriptures together as a family is a very
cohesive activity. We like doing this as a family.

Gina Woolf

When I have a family, I want to do family council
once a month. We will gather as a family and discuss
anything that we need to. What can we improve? What
do you feel is not fair? What do you like? I want to give
kids a chance to voice their opinion.

Charla Aranda

When we move to a new home, we think about what we
want that home to provide (like warmth, learning, love,
fun, safety, etc.) We type up a little statement of those
ideas, hang it by the door, and say a prayer together
as a family to give thanks for the home the Lord has
provided for us.

Alaina Jensen

Every night before bed we gather together and read
from the scriptures and say a family prayer. Sometimes
it's late and we can only read one verse, other nights
we read a chapter, but it has become a tradition to read
every night.

Sally Bender

When I was young, my mom and dad set a goal for us to read the Book of Mormon once each year. We took turns reading each night and our testimonies grew. We not only grew individually, but through the power of the scriptures, we grew closer together in love.

Janae Piercy

Ideas for your family tradition:

_____

_____

_____

_____

_____

Service Traditions

My church has a biannual conference that is
broadcasted on television, so a few weeks before
conference weekend, my family identifies a need that
we have noticed in the world. We then order supplies,
and on conference weekend we put together something
to respond to that need. For example, last conference
weekend we ordered supplies and on the Saturday
of conference we put together 144 hygiene kits for
the humanitarian aid department of the church. We
delivered them later that week with our kids and gave
them a tour of the humanitarian aid department and
let them see all the places these kits could go and could
be used for. Next conference we are looking at doing
the newborn infant kits and sending them to Haiti.

Renee Farris

We wanted to sponsor a child through Save the
Children. Our budget was tight and we wanted to have
each of our children feel that they were helping to
sponsor this child too. So, we economized by having
soup for dinner every Tuesday.

Steve and Diane Huyett

Also, we sort of adopted the Association for Retarded
Citizens as an organization we could do family service
for. We ask them what needs to be done, and then
we do it. We have painted rooms, refinished lunch
tables, pruned the garden, etc. This tradition taught
Christian principles like giving back to the community,
compassion for the less fortunate, and the joy that
comes from doing service.

Steve and Diane Huyett

We use a calendar as a service chart to mark one form of service we did that day.

Malorie Lifferth

As an extended family, every other year we try to do a service at Christmas like making humanitarian kits.

Tamra Lybbert

When a friend or someone at church had a baby, my family would make a quilt for that baby. We would all get together as a family and watch a movie together as we quilted together.

Janae Piercy

When someone is sick in my family, there is a standard procedure that is strictly adhered to. One family member is designated "the nurse" and they are to take care of the "patient." When the sick one wants something, they use my mom's Tinkerbell bell to call the nurse in for a drink or whatever they need. Another tradition for when we are sick is homemade oatmeal. Whenever I was sick as a kid, I always remember my mom making homemade oatmeal with apples for me. I swear it makes me feel better whenever I feel sick. I like these traditions because we learned how to be compassionate and to focus on others instead of ourselves.

Janae Piercy

Ideas for your family tradition:

_____

_____

_____

Physical Activity
Traditions

Every May we do Race for the Cure. Eight years ago in May, my mom was diagnosed with breast cancer. After surgery and a year of chemotherapy, she was a survivor! To celebrate, every May my entire family walks or runs a 5K for Race for the Cure. Now there are twenty-three of us. Some run and some push the strollers with the grandkids but we all participate to show our support and give back to those helping with cancer research. We do it to show our appreciation for my mom still being here today.

Crystal Howarth

My dad has been practicing karate since he was around twenty years old, and he has had all of his kids train from the time they're toddlers (or younger) until they are near college age at least. One tradition was a game he would play with us: he would sit in on the ground in front of one of us and put out either his left hand or his right hand. We would try to kick it before he pulled it back. He would gradually increase the speed. So he used to invent fun little games like that to get us excited about working out.

Nathan Bench

We go on walks around the neighborhood Sunday evenings after eating Sunday dinner together. I can't remember us not doing this. Nowadays, it is often just my dad and one or two other people. I remember some of the best conversations with my dad happened on these walks.

Jenna Kimble

My family trains for a triathlon each summer. So far it is just my wife and I, but when we have kids we would like them to also be involved. It feels amazing to be in shape and it is just a great bonding experience. It also does not take up all our free time year round because it is just once a year, so we just prepare for a couple of months.

Jared Hulme

My family lives on an island, and on Sunday evenings we would go sailing in our small Santa Cruz 27' in the Puget Sound. Those were some of the only times when we would really get to interact with each other in the quiet outside air.

Morgan Gibbons

One tradition we have is to go skiing pretty much every year during the Christmas break. We love skiing together because it is such a good bonding time and it is so fun and beautiful to be outdoors. It's fun to be bundled up in the car together in our ski clothes, to be exhausted on the way home, to have races, to find new paths in the trees, and to become better friends.

Sierra Wilson

My family does Tennis Tuesdays! We have a family tennis match every Tuesday, and the winners get Dairy Queen. Also, we plan a hike every year (Grand Canyon, Mt. Whitney, etc.), and we add the pictures to our "hiking" scrapbook.

Malorie Lifferth

Ideas for your family tradition:

_____

_____

_____

_____

_____

Work and Chores
Traditions

WORK AND CHORES

I loved doing yard work Saturday morning as a family.
Stacey London

We like to get everyone together and go room by room
to clean things. We turn on Abba or European Polka
hits or the Newsies soundtrack—whatever we can sing
to or really move to. Mom would read out loud to us
while we folded the laundry. We went through lots of
books that way, and we wanted to get more laundry
to do so we could hear more of the story. We actually
wanted to get the work done, and had fun doing it. My
mother was brilliant!
Lisa Nielson

We have a system for doing dishes. Each child has to
unload half a tray of the dishwasher. Then for loading
the dishwasher, each has to load two times his age-
worth of dishes. My seven year old has to load fourteen
dishes. Pots count for three dishes, or if it's really dirty
it will count for five.
Gina Woolf

We didn't really do chores during the week, but
Saturday was chore-day. Mom would write down a list
of everything that needed to be done and we would
write our name next to the jobs we wanted to do. Then
we'd get everything done while listening to the Aladdin
soundtrack! Typically those who finished first would
help the others so that we could finish faster and go
play.
Sabrina Huyett

WORK AND CHORES

It was a policy in our house that when we were old enough to have our learner's permit, in order to "pay" for our driving insurance, we had to wash the minivan once a month. When my older brothers were old enough to drive, I usually went out and gave them a hand in washing the car.

Stacey London

When I was growing up, I would go with my dad every Saturday and mow the lawn in front of the church building. Afterward, we would go to Arby's and get roast beef sandwiches. It was a great bonding time with my dad.

Corbin Miller

When Mom is going to have a baby, we spend almost every Saturday doing chores wearing heavy backpacks on the front of our bodies to remind us not to complain to Mom—she's got it so much worse.

Malorie Lifferth

We had Friday chores. This was when all the kids would help with cleaning the house after school. Why not Saturday? Because Saturdays were more for family activities which could be simply fixing things, or shopping, but also for going places together until the kids got older and too busy.

Ruth Hammer

My mom and dad assigned each of us to have a dish day because there were seven family members.

Ariel Bean

When I was younger, we had a huge family garden that we planted and harvested together. It was fun because we got yummy fresh fruit and vegetables, but more importantly, we grew closer together and got to learn how to work hard.

Janae Piercy

Back in the good old days of Piercy Farms, my extended family would get together around harvest time to can apple and grape juice from the grapes and apples from our own orchards. We would go to my dad's shop and assign each person a job. We would all work together to make marvelous juice that we would enjoy for the coming year. There were a lot of young kids and inexperienced canners, so it was always chaos, but a fun chaos for sure!

Janae Piercy

Ideas for your family tradition:

_____

_____

_____

_____

_____

Mealtime Traditions

My friend has a tradition that during the week, the kids take turns planning dinner with mom. They get to help her make it and spend one on one time with mom in the kitchen.

Charla Aranda

When I was growing up my mom made some beef stew. She accidently forgot to take the bay leaf out before serving it to us. You can imagine our horror and surprise upon finding a plant in our stew. My mom, was quick thinking on this one and said that it was a lucky leaf and that whoever finds it gets to make a wish. It became an instant tradition that whenever you find a bay leaf in your meal you get to make a wish. I do it with my kids and they absolutely love it.

Paige Guymon

My mom's brother lived in Germany. When he returned home, he brought the tradition of saying "Have a good meal" in German after blessing the food. We started doing it too, but switched languages as various family members have lived overseas or as we've had foreign guests. I believe we have said that (or something like it) in Italian, Finnish, Dutch, Norwegian, Portuguese, Spanish, and are currently on Japanese.

Rebecca Williams

Every Sunday night is "brinner:" breakfast for dinner.

Sarah DeVore

Every Saturday Daddy cooks eggs andpotatoes for breakfast.

Alaina Jensen

Every Sunday we have hamburgers for dinner and eat popcorn at night.

Casey Knecht

In my family, every Sunday night we eat dumplings for dinner.

Daphna Zohar

For a number of years, we had tacos every Monday night for dinner. It was one of our favorite meals, and something that all of the kids would actually eat.

Megan Baker

For special occasions (and then some), Mom makes "Mom's Rolls" and our family's version of "Fruit salad."

Ariel Bean

When I was younger we started a tradition of eating grilled cheese sandwiches as a family every Sunday after church for lunch. Over the years this tradition evolved and now we eat Norwegian waffles. Norwegian waffles are thin—a little more like crepes. You can eat them plain, with butter, with homemade jam, with powdered sugar, or however you like. It is a loving time to be with family and friends on Sunday and a way to enjoy a simple but unique meal.

Sierra Wilson

After church on Sunday we all get together and make
dinner, usually something involving potatoes, meat,
and vegetables. As soon as dinner was ready we'd pray
and then eat. Toward the end of the meal we'd go over
the calendar for the week and figure out who could go
to which activities and which ones were important for
us all, as a family, to go to. Then we'd talk about what
each of us had learned in church that Sunday. This
would always lead to hours of discussion on topics
about church, school, and usually stories from Mom
and Dad's childhood. We'd clean as we talked and then
sit around the table for an hour or two. Sometimes
Sunday dinner was the only time that week we'd all be
together at the same time for more than a prayer before
bed.

Molly Peters

My mom always made hamburgers on Saturday night.
We had chips and cinnamon rolls to go with it. I always
looked forward to that.

Steve Huyett

Since I was about seven years old we have had Ramen
(yes, as in Top Ramen) for Sunday dinner. My dad
served as a missionary in Japan and they always had
this. He started by just making it for himself, but in
the end we would all ask for some, and now it has
turned into a full-fledged family tradition. We put
bacon, vegetables, and soy sauce in it. We all eat it with
chopsticks. I love Sunday dinner!

Andrea Adams

One mother was tired of facing the daily battle of whether or not to eat chocolate that day. So, her family established the tradition of Chocolate Thursdays. Every Thursday they would bake a chocolate cake. That way you can't feel guilty making it. It's a tradition!

Liz Snyder

One family I know decided to experiment with fried foods. Every Friday they would fry whatever they wanted to eat (spaghetti included). While perhaps not the healthiest tradition, I'm sure they discovered some interesting recipes.

Liz Snyder

I loved Sundays in my home growing up. Every Sunday we would make some kind of dessert (and it usually ended up being chocolate chip cookies because those were my mom's favorites, so if you wanted any help from her you had to make what she wanted). It helped us grow closer together as kids.

Stacey London

Our son gets to choose what we make for breakfast.

Elizabeth Matheson

My husband and I are planning on starting a tradition with our kids for Family Pizza Night. We're planning on having pizza and a movie every Saturday night. We'll all be in our pajamas and eat on blankets on our family room floor like a big picnic!

Megan Sorenson

A family I used to babysit for did not use a normal table cloth. They had family photos on the table with a big sheet of plastic on top. It protected the wood table from spills, and was much more interesting to look at!

Sabrina Huyett

When we have time, we will eat the dinner and then light a candle for dessert and tell spooky silly stories and watch everyone's eyes get big, especially the eyes of the youngest member of the family who hasn't heard them before.

Susan Whatcott

Every Saturday Daddy makes Belgian waffles covered in strawberries and whipped cream. On Sundays we have donuts.

Anne Tsementzis

We have a red plate that says "You are Special Today" and everyday whoever is in charge of setting the table for dinner that day decides who is "special" and puts the red plate at his/her place at the table. During dinner we go around the table and each family member tells what they love about the "special" person.

Sally Bender

When I was growing up we had warm homemade cornbread for breakfast every Monday morning. Also in my family now, we have pizza every Friday night and donuts every Saturday morning.

Sally Bender

In my friend's family, their dad makes pancakes every Saturday morning for breakfast.

Sally Bender

Dad made French toast for us every Sunday for breakfast and we helped him.

Ariel Bean

We have "Crèpe Sunday", I make crepes on Sunday morning for breakfast with all kinds of fillings like pudding, strawberries, whipped cream, brown sugar and cream, powder sugar, freezer jam, hot fudge; you name it! Yum!

Tamra Lybbert

My family is known all around our area for our barbecue. My family loves to have barbecues together anytime of the year and invite friends. My dad, being the handy man that he is, made his own grill at work and we went on a special road trip to California where he's from to get Red Oak wood for his barbecue. He swears by this wood, and anyone else who has had his barbecue would agree. Our barbecue starts with dad marinating the meats, barbecuing and then all of us gorging. The rules are that the cool guys get the privilege of being my dad's apprentice barbecuers, and that no barbecue sauce is allowed on your meat because it is that good.

Janae Piercy

We usually invite another family over to eat Sunday dinner with us.

Kendel Christensen

My fiancée and I are planning on taking our kids to restaurants frequently. We will prepare them ahead of time and teach them correct etiquette, then take them to a nice restaurant. They'll have to eat dinner correctly; it'll be their big test.

Benjamin Pacini

Ideas for your family tradition:

_____

_____

_____

_____

_____

Bedtime Traditions

Bedtime can sometimes be a battle! Yet I always remember being excited to get through with changing and brushing teeth, because I loved what always came next! We little kids would run into mom's room and jump onto her bed. Before dismissing us to our rooms, mother would read us a chapter or two from whatever story we were currently reading together. *Summer of the Monkeys*, the *Narnia* series, *Amelia Bedelia*, and dozens of other books have been endeared to me because of this nightly ritual that we had. As we grew older, mother would even let us take turns reading. Eventually I grew too anxious and curious to know what would happen next, and began to read ahead on my own.

Liz Snyder

My mom would always come and goodnight us individually (yes, that did become a verb in my house!). I treasured that one on one time with her. If ever I needed to tell her something, that's when I would do it, because it was just us, and I had her attention. I also loved that she would read to me on most nights. It started when I was eight and got *Little Women* for my birthday. After finishing *Little Women,* we read the entire eight book series of *Anne of Green Gables*. It took us until I was nearly finished with high school to read the series, and I have fond memories of closing my eyes while hearing my mom read that dear book. It brought us together.

Sabrina Huyett

We are planning to read to our kids at nighttime. We will pick out chapter books and read a little bit each night.

Megan Sorenson

Most every night we read to our children. We typically read short children's books during the day and at night read a chapter book. We are reading the Laura Ingalls Wilder series now and thoroughly enjoying our time together.

Elizabeth Matheson

Ideas for your family tradition:

_____

_____

_____

_____

_____

Just Being Together
Traditions

As a family, we always really enjoyed playing games together or spending time working on a puzzle.

Stacey London

We have a big game-playing tradition. One game is called the "hat game." We sit in a circle and take turns wearing a hat, while everyone else says things they like about the person with the hat.

Rachel Cannon

We love to play games and have many time tested favorites—one we really love we call Spit In The Eye—great for all ages. We use a thimble or tiny lid if we are playing inside and a larger vessel if we are outdoors. Everyone sits in a big circle and one person writes on a hidden piece of paper an item, then announces to the group what category the word is from i.e. (item Cheerios) tell the group cold cereal-then you fill the thimble and walk around the group and let each guess in turn—the object is to not guess what is written on the hidden paper because if you do, you get spit in the eye! Some category ideas are colors, fruit, vegetables, farm animals, countries, continents, cars, people in the room, church jobs, numbers between one and twenty—use your imagination. It is very fun! We also love to put a puzzle out for everyone to work on—that was easier before grandkids.

Patsy Chatwin

My friend has a tradition that Friday night is movie and candy night.

Sally Bender

Every first Monday of the month we have a "musical" family night. We have to perform a song we learned on the piano and dad plays a song on the guitar. We vote and whoever did the best (worked the hardest that month) gets $5! The reason this is such a huge tradition for us is we are a very non-musical family.

Malorie Lifferth

As soon as the sun goes down on Sunday, we all crawl in mom and dad's bed and watch a movie together.

Malorie Lifferth

On Saturday mornings, my family would gather in our parent's bedrooms. Everyone would sit on the bed and we would talk and play for a while before we started our day.

Megan Sorenson

Over the years we have dubbed the phrase Wacky Whatcott Night. This means the kids dress up in whatever costume they want and do some kind of dance routine or silly show for us to videotape. Once we had a magician act. The favorite is to do a scene from a family favorite movie like Beauty and the Beast opening scene "Bonjour", Emperor's New Groove (you should have seen our Yzma) and dancing and acting out scenes from High School Musical!

Susan Whatcott

We enjoy playing family games together on Sunday evening. We also watch a church movie Sunday afternoon and sometimes fall asleep on the couch!

Sally Bender

Every Sunday after we come home from church we all sit around and watch our old family movies as we eat the cheese quesadillas, apples, and chicken noodle soup that Mom makes for us. Other people outside our family probably wouldn't find much interest in our movies but we get such a kick out of ourselves. I can't even name how many inside jokes my family has now just from watching our favorite family videos.

Nancy Jones

My family is really into board games. Whenever we are together, we play tons of games such as Risk, Monopoly, Curses, Scattergories and many others. Our favorites would have to be Scattergories and Guesstures, as we get to enjoy the creative talents found in our family. These are our family pastimes on Sunday nights after church and during holidays together.

Janae Piercy

My sister and I love to play and sing music together. I will play piano, and we will sing duets together. Oftentimes, my dad, mom and brothers will join in. This is one of my absolute favorite traditions, as we are all so close together and I love the power of music in bringing our family closer together.

Janae Piercy

Ideas for your family tradition:

_____

_____

Coming of Age
Traditions

When each girl in my family "came of age," my parents would take the girl out for a dinner and give her a special present. It wasn't a big celebration or anything, but it was a beautiful way for my parents to let each of us know that the changes we were going through were wonderful. I thought it was really special that my dad was there. My dad would say he didn't really know what we were going through, but that he wanted us to know he was there for us. It left a wonderful impression on me for the role of fathers and my own future husband in the life of daughters.

Molly Peters

When each of us girls turned sixteen years old, my parents bought us each a pearl ring (some were set with diamonds, some more plain, but they were all unique). They asked us each to wear it on the ring finger that would someday hold a wedding ring. The pearl is known as the "queen of gems" and takes years to form. Pearls cannot be cleaned with harsh cleansers like other gems, but by wearing it, the pearl becomes more beautiful as it absorbs natural oils from your body. My parents wanted to give us a visual reminder of not only remaining pure, but becoming more beautiful as we went through adolescence.

Jennifer Demma

When we turn sixteen, my dad gets us a ring that has our initials on it. He has one, and each of our rings is in the same style. They look kind of like the rings that kings use to seal wax, but aren't carved as deep.

Ethan Deceuster

My friend told me of a tradition in her family that you do not get to start dating until you are sixteen and then the first real date is always with a parent. You get to dress up and they do too, and you get to pick whatever you want to do, just the two of you. It always includes dinner and dessert, also your choice.

Kellyn Humphries

This is my favorite tradition, and it is not linked to any special holiday. A very smart, caring mom shared it with me years ago. She said when my daughter got to be thirteen that it was time to celebrate her becoming a woman and to have a mother-daughter weekend alone. Every year my daughter and I go away somewhere for a full weekend of one on one girl time. We love it so much and I truly think it has been a major reason for why we are like sisters and best friends today. We have gone to Julian, Idyllwild, Downtown San Diego, Old Town, Dana Point, and even an extravagant two and a half week trip to Ireland, just the girls.

Now when my son hit thirteen, my husband started doing the same for him. They even spent four years splitting up legs across Route 66. It has been a wonderful experience for all of us. Thirteen is a tricky age for parents and teenagers and it gave us time to bond and share life experiences without the interruptions of everyday life.

Sandy Piperato

When we were old enough, Dad taught us how to drive by taking us 4x4ing out in the forest in our Suzuki. My parents love the outdoors, and the way Dad shares this love with us is by taking us 4x4ing in the Tahuya Forest near our home in Washington State. Because the forest is private property, we can legally drive there with or without a license. So, it was natural for my dad to pass on his love of off-roading to help prepare us for driving on the road. As each child in my family enrolled in driver's education courses, my dad would take the child who was learning to drive out in the forest. It is scary and thrilling to be in the car with a new driver at the wheel, and my father took the opportunity to teach us driving safety along the way; he knew it was desperately needed.

Ariel Bean

When my sister and I each turned sixteen, our first date was with our dad. On our birthday, he took us out to the Davenport, a really nice restaurant in downtown Spokane. We would eat there and get to have one on one time with our dad. It was great because my dad is such an amazing person and I love spending time with him, and he treated us like princesses. Whenever I try to tell him that he is pampering me too much, he says, "You're worth it." This date and my dad's expression of love for his daughters is very touching and I am grateful to have such an awesome dad.

Janae Piercy

Coming of Age

A family I know gets together and decides when children have proven their maturity. When a child does so, he or shoe goes to a family council with only the parents and the children who have already proven their maturity. The council gives the new adult specific duties, responsibilities, and freedoms that the other children don't have yet. I thought it was really cool, and so I would like to expand it.

I really like the idea of having my children go through rites of passage. My fiancée and I are still talking about how we are going to do it, but here's what we are thinking. When they are five years old, they will have their first task. There are a few things I could do. I could take them out to ice cream and have them do the ordering and paying. At the end they will feel a sense of accomplishment and have confidence in themselves and in me as a parent. The next rite of passage might come when they are eight years old, and other possible rites may come at twelve and sixteen years of age.

The last rite of passage won't come at a certain age—it will be whenever the adults in the family feel that the person is ready to be considered an adult. When that rite happens, the child will be recognized as an adult and given more autonomy. Perhaps he won't have a curfew anymore, etc.

Anonymous

When getting a driver's license in my family, you get the fun experience of hanging out with dad. My dad has trained seven kids to drive, as well as hundreds of fire fighters on command rigs and other big fire trucks. Thus, he is amazingly calm when an anxious and inexperienced sixteen-year-old driver comes up to the steering wheel. To get in our hours to pass the driving test, we have done road trips to Canada and to skiing mountains to get the hours in. We enjoyed it because we got to spend quality time with our dad and were able to relax while learning to drive.

Janae Piercy

Ideas for your family tradition:

_____

_____

_____

_____

_____

Miscellaneous
Traditions

Occasionally when my mother didn't want to deal with rowdy children following her around the grocery store, she would send us on a quest. If we could find grocery products that started with the letters A-Z (we could skip two or three of the harder letters) before she finished grocery shopping, she would buy us a special treat. It made shopping trips more fun for us children, and less stressful for our poor mother!

Elizabeth Snyder

If you spoil Santa Claus, the Easter Bunny, the Tooth Fairy, etc. for one of the younger kids, then that figure does not come and give you presents the next year, because it "doesn't exist."

Claire

My friend's family has a tradition that the parents give their kids a video camera as a present at their high school graduation, so they can record their memories and experiences from then on.

Charla Aranda

One of my favorite traditions is in the summer every day after lunch my mom would read to us outside.

Liesl Marshall

My friend has a tradition that they make at least one family music video a year.

Charla Aranda

My mom has a huge roll of 3' paper that she uses to make signs out of and hangs on our fireplace for special occasions: "Congratulations" for winning a track race, "Welcome Home" from college, birthdays, "good luck", etc.

Malorie Lifferth

Another running joke is whenever someone in our family is being really weird, we call them Ramone. Ramone is the official name for the black sheep of our family, and the title rotates, as we are all a little quirky

Jenna Kimble

We saved all of our elementary school artwork and now they are framed on the walls in our family room. Also, my mom is also from the Philippines, so we would have culture days and cook Filipino food. Also, anytime we painted rooms, we kids would first get to paint whatever we wanted on the walls, and then paint over it together.

Jessie Evans

My husband will pay the kids a couple bucks to rub his feet or back.

Lacey Charlesworth

In our house when you lose a tooth you may write a letter to the tooth fairy and put it under your pillow along with the tooth.

Anne Tsementzis

My parents never let us leave to go somewhere without saying "I love you." Once when I was in middle school, I was angry and ran out to the bus without saying anything. Later that morning, I got called down to the school office. My mom was on the phone, and had called to say she loved me. This is a tradition that I know I'll carry on to my family.

Rebecca Williams

Every May 1, the women in my family pick flowers and put them under our pillows when we go to sleep. The story is that, this way, we will dream of our true love. We've had very interesting dreams over the years, including one dream my sister had about Darth Vader. My sister Sarah, who was very into literature, folklore, traditions, etc., started us doing it when she was young. When she was in elementary school, a woman came to talk to them about Swedish traditions, and this was one of them.

Rachel Cannon

One of my daughters passed away, and every year on her birthday, we eat her favorite dessert—banana splits—and talk about fun memories we have of her. It has been great to let younger members of the family know her, and it has meant a lot to the rest of us, as it helps heal the broken heart. Talking about her and eating her favorite food helps her seem closer

Zada Clark

My brother-in-law makes each of his grandchildren a chair for their two-year-old birthday.

Steve Huyett

You know how it is when mother goes out of town. No one really wants to fill her shoes. Well, whenever my Aunt Colleen would go out of town, my Uncle Ron would officially declare a Festival of the Lazy People. No one was allowed to do any work outside or inside whatsoever. Not even cooking was allowed! Pizza would be ordered out, but you have to be too lazy to pick it up. It has to be delivered. Then they would just watch movies and take it easy. My sister picked up the tradition after rooming with my cousin at college. She affectionately decided to call the Festival of Lazy People "FLOP". She realized the acronym was wrong, but decided to be too lazy to fix it.

Liz Snyder

Everyone needs a little more luck in life. My cousin's family began the odd tradition of attempting to steal other people's luck. On the first of each month, they try to steal everyone's luck by being the first to say "Rabbit, rabbit, rabbit" to another. It became such a tradition in their family, that my family was soon drawn into it as well. One cousin went to call his mother on the first of the month, hoping to rabbit her before she could rabbit him. Thanks to the aid of caller-id, she simply answered the phone by saying, "Rabbit, rabbit, rabbit."

Liz Snyder

Every time one of us has a baby, my father takes us to buy a new dress—usually waiting until we are back to the size we want to be.

Jennifer Demma

We have a long standing "Cannon Family Tradition." Apparently it goes back generations. The story has it that 7th cousins on the Isle of Man are also familiar with this tradition. It goes, "Never spoil a good story for the sake of a little truth." Basically, good stories are worth a fair amount of stretching and an opportunity to share a good story should never be passed up. We kept this tradition alive by asking everyone who came to visit our house to tell us "a story we've never heard before."

Rachel Cannon

If there was ever a time we needed to pick who went first for something, whether it be the first one to open a present on Christmas, or who got to pick the treat for our family picnic, we would do the chocolate cinnamon roll. My mom would make cinnamon rolls (usually just from the package) and we would fill one of them with chocolate chips. Then whoever got that one was the lucky one! No fighting, it was all a game.

Jonathan Drysdale

With multiple children it is difficult to record everything—cute things they say or do—use your calendar—it's easy to grab a crayon and write it on the calendar—then you can transfer it to their baby books at a more convenient time—or at the end of the year when you change calendars—it's easy to forget those precious moments and when they are older, they love to read the funny things they said or did.

Patsy Chatwin

My mother died when I was a little girl, and every year
we have banana splits on her birthday to remember
her, she loved banana splits! We have ice cream cake
on my sister's birthday to remember her. My grandma's
favorite food was Mexican food, so we eat that on her
birthday. It's a fun tradition to remember loved ones
who have passed on in a special way.

Sally Bender

Our kids raised pigs, dairy calves, and steers with the
4-H club. Every year our family would take our trailer
to the county fair and live at the fair for the whole
week. Being in 4-H, we learned new skills, met new
people, learned about animals and marketing and
business skills.

Steve and Diane Huyett

To show appreciation for my mom, in addition to our
normal kitchen chores, after Sunday dinner, my mom
was sent out of the kitchen/dining room, and the rest
of the family stayed in the kitchen until everything was
cleaned - we cleared and washed the table, put away
leftovers, washed the dishes and cleaned the kitchen
counters etc.

Amy Felsted

Every time someone comes back home, my dad's side
of the family all gets together and has dinner at Round
Table Pizza. Also, if anyone leaves we get together at
Round Table. Basically, if people are coming and going
around holidays we eat there a lot!

Megan Sorenson

My mom and I have a set date for the movies on Super Bowl Sunday. Usually it is a real chick-flick packed afternoon with a nice dinner out. This gives Dad the day to host a very manly Super Bowl Party with his guy friends.

Christy Sopher

All of my brothers and sisters and I wore braces. After every orthodontist appointment my mom would take us out for frozen yogurt, McDonald's ice cream, or smoothies. She would also do this after doctor's appointments.

Nancy Jones

While most people find power outages a setback, I find them quite fun. When the power went out, my family would all gather around the dining room table and light candles (this was a special occasion in my family, as my dad is a fire chief and candles are considered contraband in our home). Then, we would play games and do things together. I always wished the power would go out again so we could all relax and play together. Those times were marked by smiles, joy, laughter and love.

Janae Piercy

Ideas for your family tradition:

_____

_____

_____

_____

Your Year of Traditions

Ideas for your birthday tradition:

_____

_____

_____

_____

_____

Ideas for your New Year's tradition:

_____

_____

_____

_____

_____

Ideas for your Valentine's Day tradition:

_____

_____

_____

_____

_____

_____

Ideas for your St. Patrick's Day tradition:

_____

_____

_____

_____

_____

Ideas for your April Fool's Day tradition:

_____

_____

_____

_____

_____